CU00418909

1 MONTH OF
FREE
READING

at

www.ForgottenBooks.com

By purchasing this book you are eligible for one month membership to ForgottenBooks.com, giving you unlimited access to our entire collection of over 1,000,000 titles via our web site and mobile apps.

To claim your free month visit:
www.forgottenbooks.com/free199866

ISBN 978-0-483-23113-9
PIBN 10199866

LIFE

IN THE

LIGHT OF GOD'S WORD:

SERMONS

BY

(Thomson)

WILLIAM LORD ARCHBISHOP OF YORK.

LONDON:

JOHN MURRAY, ALBEMARLE STREET.

1868.

PREFACE.

THE object of the present volume is to bring together discourses addressed to many congregations under very various circumstances, so as to display many of the feelings and interests of modern life, under "the light of God's word." Some of the sermons have been printed already; and others have found their place here on account of promises given that they should one day be published.

As one or two quotations from other writers are acknowledged in the notes, it might be supposed that the author owned no other literary obligations than those which are thus admitted. This is by no means the case. But the sermons were written rapidly, and for the pulpit only ; and the references, omitted as useless at the moment, could not now be supplied. The attempt would have involved more time than the author could afford, and this without doing complete justice.

If, in a time of much criticism of old ideas and beliefs, these pages should happen to supply to them that need an argument or a motive, here and there, for hope in Christ, and should aid in preventing some honest mind from sinking down in sheer perplexity, the author will have all the reward that he hopes for, and far more than he could claim.

CONTENTS.

CONDITION OF THE CHURCH.

PREACHED IN NORWICH CATHEDRAL, AT THE CHURCH CONGRESS, 1865.

" Look upon Zion, the city of our solemnities : thine eyes shall see
Jerusalem a quiet habitation, a tabernacle that shall not be
taken down ; not one of the stakes thereof shall ever be
removed, neither shall any of the cords thereof be broken : But
there the glorious Lord will be unto us a place of broad rivers
and streams ; wherein shall go no galley with oars, neither
shall gallant ship pass thereby."

A GREAT and high promise for the chosen
people is contained in these words. Jerusalem, the centre of their worship, of their religious
affections, should be at peace. Her tabernacle
should not be the tent of their old wanderings,
but a fixed abode, with stakes that should not be
removed, and cords that could not be broken. No
broad river as yet refreshed the thirsty Jerusalem ;
but the glorious God would make river and stream
to flow, and these should cheer and enrich ; but
the war-ship should not find a passage over them
to destroy. On Jerusalem, often wasted with
misery and war, often careless about God, should
shine all peace and blessing. She should be for

ever a strong city, perfect in beauty, peaceful and secure.

That this prophecy is not to be limited to the visible city of Jerusalem, its own words show. The living river shall never flow nigh her, nor a tabernacle with cord and stake replace the firm foundations of the glorious temple that was her pride already. Nor did it ever find its fulfilment in the visible Jerusalem. That city fell to the warrior, was destroyed at last in war. Her sceptre has fallen out of her hands. Her fortifications, strong and steep, became, as other prophets [1] said they would become, sloping fields of waving corn. Her stakes are removed, and her cords broken ; and no one can renew her landmarks, so that we might restore, even for our imagination, the fair city, the joy of the whole earth.

But all things urge us to give the whole section in which these words occur a larger scope. It is of a higher Zion that the prophet speaks ; of a Zion that has a corner-stone elect, precious, which never was hewn with hands from the quarry; of Zion, of which it would be said, "Thine eyes shall see the King in his beauty; they shall see the land that is far off." (Chap. xxxiii. 17.) The King is surely

---

[1] Jer. xxvi. 18 ; Mic. iii. 12.

the Anointed One for whom the nation sighed ; and the land far off is the enlarging borders of that King's dominions, which embrace not Jewry only, but the distant places of the earth, all made subject to the one King of Zion.   These promises, then, refer not to the kingdom of Hezekiah, but more truly to that Church where Christ is judge and lawgiver and king, and where the people, stricken with the sense of sin, look to Him alone, and say with the prophet, " He will save us."   The prophet sees in the foreground a king and people delivered from the fear of invasion and captivity ; and these have their place in his inspired strain of triumph.   But his vision sweeps the space beyond, pierces into the ages that shall be ; and a loftier throne and a more glorious temple, and a kingdom reaching over all the earth, grow upon his mind and claim his words.   Directed by him, the pious listeners would long for that better time which was never absent from their thoughts, which was so essential to their conceptions of God's glory and man's need.   And thus, out of the temporary distress of Zion, and her rescue from the hand of Sennacherib, rises up a larger vision, beneath which the local groups and circumstances seem to grow less, and almost to disappear.

Will it remove all difficulty from this prophecy if we apply it to the Christian instead of to the Jewish Church? I think that at a meeting like this, we shall be reminded often of the same bitter contrast between those high promises which we inherit and our actual state, which must have depressed the spirit of the Jews, when the hosts of the enemy appeared in their borders. To our Zion, to the Church of Christ, are promised explicitly such gifts as these—unity, truth, and success. Of which of them, it may be asked, can we make our boast? Which of these precious gifts do we enjoy in that large measure in which they were all promised to us? And since He is faithful that promised, what are the faults in us that bar us from our birthright? These are questions of most serious import. Let us commence the proceedings of this week by turning our minds to them for a few moments.

1. The unity of the Church was to be one chief note of its divine origin. "That they all may be one; as thou, Father, art in me, and I in thee, that they also may be one in us: that the world may believe that thou hast sent me." Here is no mere assumption that as a matter of prudence Christians will cling together; but their unity, of souls united

by an interpenetrating love, is an image of the
mysterious union betwixt the Father and the Son ;
nay, and the sight of that unity will make the
world believe that the mission of the Son was true
indeed. What is our state? Visible unity seems
to be no more a mark of the Church of Christ.
Of those whose faces are all turned one way, to
the place where Jesus the crucified sits on the
right hand of God, the east and west have been
rent asunder, so that none can re-knit the torn
garment of the Lord. And west and east are
again divided, each within itself ; and we that are
but a section of the western Church, are torn and
torn again. It is not that men are careless to preserve their inheritance, and so suffer themselves to
be separated from indifference about the value of
union. It is that the good, the pious, the zealous,
are unable to reconcile the claims of truth with
those of love ; are unable to draw the line between
zeal and severity. It is sometimes that men doubt
the power of truth in itself, and add their anger to
it to give it weight. And this root of trouble is
not of modern planting. The dispute of Paul with
Barnabas, the error of Peter at Antioch when Paul
withstood him to the face because he was to be
blamed, show us that even men the holiest, the

most fervid, the most devoted, were the first to
shake a little the stones of the new wall that was
rising about the new Jerusalem, the Church, and
that they did it with the thought that they were
doing God service. *We* dare not blame either
side, since the one aimed at strict right, the other
at charitable indulgence.   But it is remarkable
how fruitful of evil, down to this very day, was
that open rupture of Paul and Peter on account
of Peter's weakness at Antioch.   The Ebionites
founded on this their gravest accusation against
Paul ; as the Gnostics did their prejudice against
Peter and the apostles of the Jews.   The ration-
alists argue from it against inspiration ; and the
so-called critical school of the present day have
constructed upon it a theory of Church history
which supposes a constant and avowed hostility
between these two greatest apostles, commencing
at Antioch, never ending during their lives, the one
preaching a gospel strictly connected with the old
law, and the other desiring to emancipate the
Church from all traces of the law.   Of this theory,
which pretends to discover a chasm dividing the
new Jerusalem into two parts from the very first,
I will only say here, that it was a great effort of
imagination to construct it out of few materials,

and in defiance of many obvious facts, and a great
effort too to take such a dream for history. It is
without any evidence; it is against evidence. But
the sharp contention of apostles shows us already
what peril surrounds the Church, of permanent
division. Yes: the great idea of an undivided
Church, completely fused and compacted by love
and by truth, came down from heaven; but the
treasure was received in earthen vessels, which
could not contain it: the vessels broke, and the
treasure was lost. I know that the Church of
Rome insists still that visible unity is a mark of
the Church, and that she alone exhibits that mark,
and that no other Christian body separated from
her can claim the title of a Church, because it
wants one of its essential notes. But such pretensions cannot be admitted. The mirror in which
the ascended Lord was to be visibly reflected to an
admiring world has been broken to pieces. Every
fragment still reflects, but more or less perfectly,
the Lord of glory. To take up one of the pieces,
much defiled by the earth on which it has fallen,
and to set it in a gaudy frame, and to say, " This
fragment is the mirror, and all the rest are nothing," this may deceive some who yearn so much
for unity, that they would rather admit than sift the

claim. But earnest hearts sicken at the vain pretension. From east and west, in parts of which
Rome knows nothing, voices of praise arise to the
one Lord of all believers ; and works of good are
done in the name and in the power of that Lord.
The Lord is their judge, the Lord is their lawgiver,
the Lord is their king. To deny that they are
Christ's seems hardly to stop short of blasphemy
against Him whose power is seen among them.
That Rome should claim to be the sole trustee of
that precious gift, because of the mark of unity, is
indeed a bold assumption. Rome, ever more ready
to cut off than to embrace ; Rome, that would have
nothing to do with those holy aspirations after a
purer worship, and a truer teaching, which brought
round the Reformation ; Rome, like her sisters,
may muse in sorrow over Christ's promise of unity
made seeming void by man's sin. But for her, less
than for others, is the arrogant pretension that she
alone is the divine Zion, and all that she has cut
off are useless fragments, cast into the darkness.
And yet so deep-seated is the love for unity, that
many have accepted her at her word, and sought
in her bosom what she had not to give. Because
the flower is withered, they have been fain to clasp
to their bosom an artificial flower, different even

to the eye from that which it would imitate, but
without the life or the odour. All we the rest, to
whom such pretensions are an idle tale, sit brooding on the seeming frustration of a most blessed
promise. Where is the one fold, whose sheep in
one flock follow the leading footsteps of the one
Shepherd into green pastures that never fail?
God's promise cannot have been in vain. Man
must have hindered it : God hath not forgotten it.
So much the greater is our inheritance of sin, so
much the more do we need to seek wisdom and
guidance from Him whose gracious purpose we
have failed for ages to understand.

2. But if unity has been lost, truth has been
preserved to us. And this is our consolation. If
the Church be not the great ocean, vast, bright,
fresh, a counterpart of the blue heaven above it,
still she is like the hundred lakes that nestle
among the sheltering hills ; they know not each
other, but every one of them reflects, and truly, the
firmament above. So far as salvation by Christ
is brought home to men by the teaching of the
churches, so long there is an underlying bond of
agreement which outward misunderstanding cannot cancel. We are one in the one witness that
we bear to Jesus, in the one hope that we awaken

through His gospel, in the one common direction
towards which our faces turn, waiting till the dark
sky shall kindle with the orient flush of His glorious reappearing. And yet we must admit that
even here we are not safe. The world, steeped in
material things, grown rich, grown wise, and full
of enjoyment, is waking to discuss the truths of
religion. In every country almost this is the
subject of the hour. And no tenet of our holy
faith shall escape gainsaying. Such trials have
been before, and the Church has come out of them.
We do not despair; but we must be forewarned
against a state of real danger. *Do* you love the
Bible, and find it a sufficient guide? Not a book
of it shall escape some critical doubt. Do you
think your soul is precious because it lives for
ever? Materialism, with curled nostril, tells you
that all that is gone, and that when man dies he
perishes utterly. *Do* you love the Redeemer for
all that His love has done for you? New lives
have been written of Him we adore as Redeemer.
Redemption finds no place in that tangle of
enthusiasm, perplexity, and deceit, which some
would have us substitute for the living picture of
our eternal Lord. What, then, would become of
sinners without a Redeemer? Sin, too, is to be

abolished by the command of pantheism, and sin
and goodness alike are necessary manifestations of
absolute being, and it would be absurd to condemn
what is inevitable and necessary. Leave us, at
least, out of this wreck of all things, the belief that
God is the Father of His creatures, and that we
can know Him! Not so. Science forbids us to
deal but with facts of observation. For thoughts
such as yours science has no room. We do but
waste time in denying or refuting them ; they are
outside the path of reason altogether, as our dreams
are out of the course of our daily avocations. No
book to guide us ; no king to lead us ; no difference of right and wrong ; no life beyond this sick
and lame existence ; no father touched with love
for us whom we are permitted to love. Then has
winter darkness overtaken us on a bleak and windy
moor ; we must sit down in our blind despair until
the eager breeze shall search through blood and
marrow, and our torpid sleep deepen into a death
beyond what men call death. God forbid it! We
shall not utterly die in this unbelief. But short of
death we may suffer much harm and loss. And a
Church with broken love and tainted truth, what
has she to assure her that she belongs any more to
Him who sent her forth to present to the world

the image or copy of His love and zeal, and teach men all that He had commanded? It is neither an example nor a witness. What, then, is it?

3. Not less humiliating to us are those promises of great success which are a part of our charter. The power of the truth we teach, the presence of the Holy Ghost, to turn the outward Word into an inward life, seem to assure us of great success in gathering in souls to Christ. " All power is given unto me in heaven and in earth," He said, when He bade His disciples go and teach and baptize all nations; and He promised to be with them always, even unto the end of the world. If, instead of conquering evil in the heathen nations round us, through that all-powerful One who has promised to go out with us, our missions are almost standing still, and round about our doors at home much heathen ignorance prevails; if, instead of pulling down strongholds by the power of the Word, we are ourselves besieged in our Jerusalem by errors that would ruin the very foundations of our faith, here is one more disappointment, one more source of perplexity in understanding the ways of God.

Brethren, a Church Congress must take for the basis of its discussions these admitted facts of our condition : that our unity has long been broken up; that the precious truth entrusted to us is threatened ; and that because of these the work of evangelization proceeds but slowly. These facts are terrible in themselves; they are astonishing when contrasted with the large promises that attended the sending forth of the ministers of the gospel. It is essential that we should realise that the temporary failure of the divine purpose lies with man and with his sin, and not with Him who made the promise. The history of the Jewish people is but a prophecy of our own. On one side, Jehovah offered to His chosen every blessing that love could give. The tabernacle with cords and stakes that could not be moved, the streams of water to quicken their arid soil, and yet to refuse a passage to the hostile ships ; these are some of the images under which the prophets assure the people that the Lord Jehovah loves them with an everlasting, with an unsparing love. On the other hand, the chosen people, by wilful apostasy, turn aside the gracious purpose, and the great shower of blessing hangs in a cloud above them, but cannot fall on this unthankful, stiff-necked race. The pious Jew, in the decline of his country, might ponder on the long catalogue of blessings that had been promised but not sent. Were the promises but visions, that never should have been expected to issue in literal fulfilment? No. Every promise would have been performed; but the sinful will of man, impotent for good without God's help, is permitted an awful power to the prevention of good. It seems well-nigh profane to say that God cannot act out His love for man, if man resists Him; yet this is, in one sense, true and scriptural. We have heard in the lesson that "He could there do no mighty work," and unbelief was the cause. And so the words of the prophet seem for a time to fall to the ground. Just thus it is with the Church. God meant her to be a city set on a hill, strong, undivided, beautiful, presenting to an admiring world the copy of its Founder's beauty. Christ meant to be with it always, its lawgiver and king; meant that the Spirit's fire should lighten every conscience and warm every heart with the love of truth and of God. There is only one cause for His diminishing aught of His promises. Man would not have it so. The passions of our corrupt nature would not be still even in that heavenly presence, and so two apostles fall into sharp contention; and Peter vacillates and Paul denounces vacillation, even then when the

Lord is pointing them the way to gather in the Gentiles into His fold. It was ·His work. Oh, that they would have stood still to see His salvation! If those holy men, our inspired instructors in the faith, if those great spirits, consecrated to such high and elevating functions, could be ruffled into quarrel, though but for a moment, no wonder that the strife of ages less faithful, bit deeper, and made wounds that would not heal. And so the Church, founded by the Prince of Peace, has passed through eighteen stormy ages.

But God is very good to us. We are broken; our lips stammer over the truth; we labour feebly for the good of souls. Yet God is with us still. If we have refused to be blessed according to His plan, He has blessed us in another. And no Church on earth has more cause for humble gratitude than that which we claim as our own. The pure Word of God, that Word written for us in the age when the Holy Spirit was poured on the Church in largest measure, is preserved to us, is in every cottage, is learned by every child. The sacraments are still ministered to us in their original purity. There is much love amongst us, even with our strife; there is a warm and growing zeal in works of good. Without the presence of the Spirit

B

these things could not be. This great assembly, to which I am so unworthy to speak, is a proof of divine life. We have come here to seek for the wisdom that is of God; to discuss the means which, under God, may tend to restore the old unity, to preserve the old truth, to bring back to Christianity its ancient days of victory. We shall best deliberate on such high themes if we refresh our spirits with the music of those promises wherewith the Church, that should be peace on earth with the Prince of Peace to guide it, was founded at first. We shall wait for the consolation of Israel, and seek peace and treasure truth, as though eighteen centuries of disappointment had not dashed down our hopes. Of practical activity, of all the methods and devices of business, we are sure to have enough; this age abounds in them. We need to go back to that pure and holy law, given in the Sermon on the Mount, true from everlasting, with its blessings for the merciful and the seeker after peace, even though many of us that are Christians cannot lift ourselves up to its level, could not breathe in that rare atmosphere of perfect self-negation. We ought to long for a time, and pray for it, when the earth shall be full of the knowledge of the Lord as the waters cover the sea; even though practical men (so they are called) shake their heads at what they call a visionary hope. We shall not see it. If all the powers in earth, civil and ecclesiastical, were to enact that Christendom should be at one, it would burst the enforced bond, and crumble again into the old divisions, because the blending and combining spirit was not there. But by looking to what the Church was meant to be at first, we shall best bring our own branch of the Church into the state in which Christ would have it. And nowhere else could such an effort be made more hopefully. We have sinned and strayed; but what other Church can cast the first stone at us? Of increasing love and unity this meeting is one sign among many. Those painful errors of doctrine, to which I alluded, grow rankest on foreign soil; the pest that threatens the lambs of our fold is wafted to us from over the sea. Our interest in missions abroad, in education at home, is a thing of yesterday; but it grows.

Carry we this spirit into our councils this week, dear friends, the spirit that yearns for union and hates division, that will keep and speak the truth, but always in love, that knows it must work ever towards that consummation of the Church whereof

the patent tokens are but few. Let no sharp contention check our affectionate intercourse; let no
despair prevent us from encouraging attempts at
good. When the spirit of unity, of truth, and of
zeal, is strong in our hearts, we shall be sure that,
though the Church lie long in ruins, we are made
by that spirit lively stones, fit to be used to build
it again. For not one promise of Jewish prophet,
of apostles, or of the Lord himself, shall in the end
be found to have perished. We have put back the
hand upon the dial, but it moves, and it shall one
day strike. Jerusalem was founded that there
might be " salvation in Zion for Israel my glory ; "
but unfaithfulness wearied the Lord, and He gave
it to the spoiler. The Church was founded a
second time, but she has never claimed her own,
has never moved to follow her Lord but with lame
and crippled feet. Yet shall there be a third Zion,
a new Jerusalem, wherein all the promises of God
shall meet, and the wealth of His goodness shall
be fully seen. If this state through which we are
passing continues to disappoint our hopes, by
striving to live above it, we are preparing for that
sweet and blessed country into which all of us
shall come. Yes! the vision of that future glory
of our Lord is needed to keep up our hearts, is

needed for a right conception of Him ; not always baffled and refused by men, not always forbearing and holding back. Christ shall one day be universal king. Clouds are about those prophecies, but the life-giving sun is behind them. The manner may be dark, but the thing shall be. All of us shall hear what the apostle heard in his vision : "There were great voices in heaven, saying, The kingdoms of this world are become the kingdoms of our Lord and of His Christ, and He shall reign for ever and ever." Blessed are we, if we can then say, "Lord, we have watched and waited and longed for Thy kingdom, even whilst men slumbered and slept, because the Bridegroom tarried : take us in with Thee !"

II.

THE THOUGHT OF DEATH.

PREACHED IN GLOUCESTER CATHEDRAL ON THE DAY OF
THE FUNERAL OF THE PRINCE CONSORT,
DECEMBER 23, 1861.

"Dust thou art, and unto dust shalt thou return."

IT is not often, my friends, that we witness the grand spectacle of a national sorrow. When a great man is called away, we sometimes speak of his removal as a national calamity, but our grief comes rather from reflection than from feeling; and we say we are sorry when we mean that we ought to be so. But this is not so now. We feel our grief as well as think it. We never pronounce the name of him that God has taken away without feeling the heartache of a personal loss; nay, when the name is only missed—when in our Church Service its absence abates the loyal prayer for the first family in the land, I have felt that a thrill went through the congregation, as though we suddenly missed a familiar friend. We may be proud of the people that has in it such a fund of loyal affection; we may be thankful for the virtue in high places that has drawn upon that affection so deeply. But there are other thoughts for us at present. I invite you to stand by the grave of a great prince, and read again the old lesson, that we must all die. I invite you to learn the old wisdom that the grave teaches. The dust sounds hollow as it falls on the coffin lid ; and this is the word it speaks—*Dust thou art, and unto dust shalt thou return.*

Brethren, let us once more read that trite lesson —the reality of death. All of us who are met together here shall face that terror and fight that conflict; all the upturned faces that I see before me in this church shall one day be turned towards the judgment-seat of Christ.

1. Men know not that they shall die, even though they confess it with their lips almost daily. If we consider what death is, we see that men that *know* its approach will act in all things as in the fear of it. It must be the first thought of the day; it must be the thought with which the eyes close for sleep. "From my little hoard of days, which I am not suffered to count, one more is taken away. One more fragment of my time broken off, and cast into the abyss of eternity behind me. And when the tale of my days is told out, I too shall pass into that unexplored eternity." Are these

the thoughts with which men wake from their sleep? The condemned criminal in his cell does so, for he can count on the fingers of one hand the days that still interpose between him and the dust of death; and even he does not leave hope till the last weak chances of a reprieve have been exhausted. But men in general die suddenly, not thinking of death at all. I do not say men die in a moment. The thunderbolt shall not strike them. Their ship shall not be shattered on an inhospitable shore, that the white sea, lashing itself to madness, may devour them. No tower of Siloam need fall on them to crush out their life. They are safe from the shock of the battle: they escape the sudden pestilence. They are carried about on wheels that outstrip the tempest; and neither spring, nor rail, nor signal, betrays them to swift death. Many a precious life is lost to us by such means. But these deaths are not the only sudden ones: nay, for the man of faith and prayer the most sudden stroke of death is never unexpected, even though he pass out of sleep into eternity. But men that die in their beds of gradual sickness, die suddenly, when they have to face a judgment which they have never thought about or lived for. When the physician says to them—" Set thine

house in order, for thou shalt die, and not live,"
even the worldly matters in which they have been
engrossed are all unfinished and unprepared. Time
is too short for all that has to be crowded into it.
The feeble and wandering brain collects itself to
dispose in haste of all its possessions to others.
In health not one-hundredth part of those treasures had passed from the hands without far more
circumspection and misgiving than now can attend
the transfer of the whole. Writings intended for
no human eye but one, are left unburnt in the
desk : old strifes and sorrows will be exhumed, by
the hands of the heir, out of papers long destined
to the fire. Children are summoned from afar to
hear counsels and wishes that would have been
given them long ago, if death had been thought of
in earnest. And before the last wishes can be
hurried through, night gathers over the eyes, and
the breath comes hard, and the pulse flutters and
stands still. If it is so with our worldly affairs, it
will not be better with the things that belong to
the soul. In the midst of pleasures, in the hurry
of engrossing business, in the delights of study
and self-cultivation, something that we feel within
us gives us the warning to set our house in order.
The life of this world is over ; what have we done

to prepare for another? Is it possible that we
have done nothing? Have we given all the hours
wherein we calmly possessed our strength, to utter
worldliness of spirit, and now are we obliged to
turn to God when death has already stricken us,
and to offer Him the dregs of our cup of life, and
prepare for heaven in the midst of our terror, and
hurry, and exhaustion? Then we did not surely
believe in death; we never thought of that baptism
wherewith we must all be baptized. It has come
upon us suddenly now, even though our disease
shall be lingering, and the days of suffering many.
Death is sudden wherever man is unprepared.

And there is no more startling paradox in the
wonders of our nature than this, that men in
general are thoughtless about death. Every week
the deaths in this country outdo the slaughter of
a battle. Wherever a thousand men are gathered
together, we may say that it is probable that ere
another year comes round, twenty-five of them
will have passed from time to eternity. Not the
oldest nor the youngest, not the good nor the bad,
not the most useless nor the most useful, lives
shall be cut off. Two sisters shall be growing, like
twin-buds upon a single stalk; "the one shall be
taken and the other left." Here an old man shall

be spared, though his life has become labour and sorrow: there the strong man in his prime, carrying succour to many, bearing good fruit now and giving presage of better, is cut down. And we sit here, if conscious at all, only dimly conscious of these terrible facts, like a flock of sheep that know not why one of their number has been snatched off by the hand that is to slay it. Yet when our turn comes, and there is no escape; when all the treasures of the mine would not buy another year of life, or persuade the disordered mechanism of our bodies to work one year longer ere it breaks down, then the terror is great and real. For the valley of the shadow of death is ever dark; and the gates of eternity are awful. Then, for the first time, we really believe in death. The illusions wherewith we kept out the thought are scattered ; and we know that it is indeed a fearful thing to die.

2. It is a fearful thing, because of the great change that it implies in all our being. Life is that power by which we act and think, and love, and intend, and hope. And suppose that all our energies have been wasted on things that cannot follow us into the grave, then how can we conceive of any life at all beyond this?

Life itself we cannot define ; that has been tried
a hundred times by men of science without success.
But we can describe its functions ; and we can
ask ourselves how many and which of these can
go on apart from this sun-lighted globe whereon
we live, apart from the conveniences and ornaments of this great country, apart from those
senses of touch, and taste, and sight, which we
pamper only too much. And when all these are
deducted, many a man will find that his whole
life is gone, that there is nothing left which he
can conceive of as going on before the throne of
eternity, where saints made perfect shall utter
everlasting praise to the thrice-holy God. He
will be unable to believe in an immortality which
he cannot even conceive. A life without money,
or feasting, or ambition, or pleasant books, or the
dance, or the spectacle, or the betting-book, or
the maddening cup, would be no life at all to one
who spends all his powers on these things only.
" If ye live after the flesh ye shall die," says the
apostle. Death looks like death indeed, if whilst
we say our soul shall live we cannot even propose
anything for it to do. A soul locked in the fetters
of an eternal idleness, brooding on the recollection
of all past pleasures, now impossible ; and chiding

the slow-rolling wheels of eternity which come ever round and round upon their unchanging axles again, bringing with them no light, no life, nothing to do and nothing to hope ; that would of itself be hell, without the torment that shall be added for the hours wasted in wickedness. No wonder that, at the sight of that baptism of death, men's souls feel straitened and oppressed. It extinguishes so much of us : it spares so little. The darkness of the valley is so thick. The strongest limbs and the most beautiful faces shall turn to a heap of loathsome dust. The artless tongues of children shall make us no more music. The rival that we strove with in our profession or our trade shall have the arena to himself. The sweet sunshine and the bracing sea-breeze shall not penetrate to the narrow house wherein our straitened limbs are sleeping with the worm. The house we built and decorated for ourselves shall be for others to dwell in. And when we know that we must die, we feel about for something in us that shall not perish ; some thread of continuity to knit our present and our future life into one ; and if we have never prayed to our eternal and invisible Lord, never lived for God, never mortified the deeds of the body through the help of the Spirit, never realised

the difference between treasures of earth and treasures of heaven, never thought of a judgment-day,
and tried our actions as though the Judge of
Quick and *D*ead saw them already, we find nothing that shall assure us of that other life. We
start back in horror from a grave so dark and so
profound. *D*eath shall not merely strip us, it shall
arrest every current of our life, and stop up every
channel. "There is no work, nor device, nor knowledge, nor wisdom, in the grave, whither thou goest."
" The dead," says *S*olomon in another place, " know
not anything, neither have they any more a reward ; for the memory of them is forgotten. Also
their love, and their hatred, and their envy, is now
perished ; neither have they any more a portion
for ever in any thing that is done under the sun."
(Eccles. ix. 5, 6.)

3. These, then, are two things which make death
terrible ; it is unforeseen, and it is an utter change
of all we know and love. If these two terrors were
all, some at least would not fear to die—would
even court death as a repose. " There the wicked
cease from troubling, and there the weary be at
rest. There the prisoners rest together ; they hear
not the voice of the oppressor." On many the load
of life sits heavy. They wrestle with poverty and

are overcome. *D*isease turns their nights into vigils of pain. The grave has swallowed up already almost all those whom they loved best. If death were a mere sleep, they would gladly lay down their heads and die. But there is yet another terror. *D*eath means judgment. To die is to meet God. "It is appointed unto men once to die, but after this the judgment." (Heb. ix. 27.) When *S*olomon says of the dead that they know not anything, neither have any more a reward, he speaks of human knowledge, and of rewards such as men strive after here below. But conscience has been whispering to us that our God, whom we have been defying, is just, and that as nothing escapes the vigilance of His power, so no sin of ours can escape from His omniscient memory. Often in our own minds acts that we had for years forgotten are called up from a deeper depth in our memory than we knew of; impressions which seemed lost were in fact only buried under a crowd of other thoughts, and what was wanting to our recollection was not so much the image of the fact as our power to recall it at will. But the prophetic vision tells us of a memory from which nothing slips away; all is written in the book of God. "I saw the dead, small and great, stand before God; and the books were opened : and another book was opened, which is the book of life : and the dead were judged out of those things which were written in the books, according to their works." (Rev. xx. 12.) He who came as the lamb to save you will judge you, if you repent not, with the wrath of the lion. And you knew it. The shame you felt at the act of impurity was a witness that you knew its foulness and its guilt. The laws men have made against sin by common consent, expressed to you that there was a right and wrong ; and your conscience never denied it. All along you felt that a mark was set upon sin. And now that you see that it was God that planted the shame in you, and the self-reproach for sin, and the admiration of what is right, you cannot complain. You felt the presage of His judgment when conscience pricked you. And now, compelled by the nearness of death to deal truly with yourself, you cannot pretend that God would set the mark of His anger on sin in this world, and in the next would make no difference between sin and righteousness. And you tremble because you shall appear before a Judge of infinite power, whose wrath no man can resist, before a Judge of infinite wisdom, who shall call back your acts out of the distant past, and lay bare the secret thoughts of your spirit. And you say, "Who may abide the day of His coming, and who shall stand when He appeareth?"

These, then, are the terrors of death to an unprepared mind; it will take a man away suddenly; it will wrest from him all that he lived for; it will introduce him at once into the presence of a Judge, in whose hands are the power of eternal life and death. I said that the thoughtlessness of most men about death was the strangest feature in our mental constitution. All must be baptized with this baptism; and yet the common object of all would seem to be to avoid all thought of it till it comes. When the idea crosses us that life is short, we argue that our health at least is sound—that our race lives to a ripe old age—that on a calculation of averages we have ten or fifteen years before us, in which we may set our house in order. With arguments as slight as these is the one great reality of life put aside, the one great work of life left undone, the one great terror of life suffered to come nearer and nearer, until it breaks forth at last upon our amazed spirit, and finds it incapable of seeking peace from God! Brethren, let us escape from this folly. The example of Him who

suffered for us will guide us in the way. Was not
He straitened or oppressed by the baptism through
which He had to pass? Was not the cup prepared
for Him of the Father bitter to drink? Was not
death terrible to one who saw its coming so clearly
long before? Were not the sins of all men grievous
to be borne? And what was it that sustained Him,
and made the seen terror and the felt guilt endur-
able? He himself tells us. He says, " I have
glorified thee on the earth. I have finished the
work which thou gavest me to do." He was oppressed because He yearned to see the Father's
will completed wholly, and at the same time shrank
with a man's weakness from the valley of the
shadow of death. In the dark struggle of Geth-
semane Satan came back to Him. The sorrows
of hell compassed Him about, and the snares of
death prevented Him. Dimly we see that here the
powers of darkness were allowed once more to
assail Him, through this fear of death—this man-
like shrinking from suffering. All in vain. Dearer
to the Son of God is it to do the will of the Father,
than to possess his human life in safety and in
peace. He will spare no fibre of His tender frame.
He will not throw off one of the sins the weight of
which He was appointed to bear. He will avoid

no circumstance of His unheard-of death. Try that death, I pray you, by the standard of a man ; for the Son of God did not act a semblance of death, but really died our death, and felt our pains. He died amidst the curses and revilings of those He came to save. Pouring out love on all men, He was repaid with hatred. Pains even like those of the Cross might have been easier to bear, had they been suffered in the midst of a thankful people, sympathizing with His anguish, and kneeling in adoration of their King, who had wrought so great a miracle of love. But forsaken of all men—asking even the Father why He had forsaken Him, the Redeemer passed beyond the reach of His tormentors. *Do* we dare to suppose that even for a moment the victory against *S*atan was doubtful. No. He was eager that His baptism of death should be accomplished. It was His strength to be able to say, "I have glorified thee on earth. I have finished the work that thou gavest me to do."

And let this mind be in you, brethren, which was in Christ Jesus ! It is no blasphemy to bid *you* glorify God on the earth, and finish the work which He gives you to do. Accept the salvation

purchased for you with His Passion; lay hold
upon the offered forgiveness; and from this
moment begin to live for God. See the days of
your life which you now scatter in trifles as an
awful trust committed to you. Give them back
to the God who lent them to you; try to render
up the precious deposit with usury. Say to yourselves daily, "I must work the work of Him that
sent me while it is day; the night cometh when
no man can work." *D*eath cannot then come
suddenly upon you, for the thought of it has
sobered all your days. It will be bitter to part
from children and friends, and to leave your
dearest undertakings to others to finish; but
still, death will not be the utter extinction of all
your pursuits, for you have begun to delight to
do the Father's will, and whatever else shall
taste corruption, that thought — that purpose—
came down from heaven : and you shall carry it
back to heaven with you again. The day of
account will still be terrible; but the belief that
you are reconciled to God through the blood of
Jesus, and that He is your Advocate with the
Father, who will be your Judge hereafter, will
sustain you. "Yea, though I walk through the

valley of the shadow of death, I will fear no evil ;
for thou art with me. Thy rod and thy staff they
comfort me."

And these more consoling thoughts are not
foreign to the sad solemnity of this day. A great
loss has fallen on us. "It is," to use words which
have been before many eyes, " it is the loss of a
public man, whose services to this country, though
rendered neither in the field of battle nor in the
arena of crowded assemblies, have yet been of
inestimable value to this nation—a man to whom,
more than to any one else, we owe the happy
state of our internal polity ; and a degree of
general contentment, to which neither we nor
any other nation we know of ever attained before."[1] And we do justice by our sorrow to
the greatness of our loss. But we are not near
a grave that a Christian shrinks from contem-
plating. There is sorrow for us ; for him there
is not fear. The grave closes to-day not over a
career of laziness, or lust, or selfish pride. His
deathbed was not the last scene of an empty
court-pageant. His life was spent in all that
gives dignity to manhood ; he filled his high,
and in a sense, irresponsible position, as know-

[1] *Times.*

ing that he, like the meanest man amongst us, was responsible before the awful tribunal of God himself for every hour spent here below. If it had not been so, you would not have come here, to this church to-day, to celebrate in grief, deep and real, his obsequies. If it had not been so, I would not have stood before you here. But I ask you to look back upon his life, pure, simple, and active, upon his unostentatious piety, upon his zeal for the public good, that your sorrow may not be that of men who sorrow without hope. Look at the boy, spending his time not "in lust, or toys, or wine," but in studies as severe as though his life depended on success in some profession. Look at the peaceful home that he made for our beloved *Sovereign*; in which the utmost research of gossips has detected nothing but purity, and goodness, and domestic peace. Look at the scrupulous care, a care far more tender and thoughtful than most fathers in any rank of life know how to exercise, with which he has guided the education of his eldest son. Look how he, to whom alone the doors of official employment have been shut, has made himself (to borrow a phrase) Minister of Civilisation in this country. There was no subject

in which honest Englishmen take an interest, that
did not at some time or other waken his interest
too.   Alike the propagation of the gospel, and the
improvements of the arts of life, alike the interests
of soul and body, quickened in his heart the sym-
pathetic pulses, and received from his tongue the
aid of no unskilful advocate.   All is taken from us,
and we try to say, " It is the Lord, let him do what
seemeth him good."   The Christmas holly shall
hear no laughter; the new year shall only revive
the recollection of what the old year has buried
from us.   There was to be a bridal in that august
house; they have ceased to weave wreaths for the
bride, and are busy over her mourning weeds.
There was to be rejoicing when an ingenuous son
should come of age; our joy is turned to sorrow,
and the son must hasten into manhood that he
may sustain a widowed mother in her cares.   A
great palace of industry was to have been opened
under the auspices of the lost one; we that witnessed that same solemnity eleven years before
will have to mourn the absence of the life and the
head of it.   Greatest sorrow of all, the Queen, the
ruler of this proud country, the most beloved sovereign of it that history wots of, is a broken-hearted
widow woman, seeking on her knees this day con-

solation from her God. It is all dark and bitter.
Yet it is the funeral of the good. " I heard a voice
from heaven, saying unto me, Write, Blessed are
the dead which die in the Lord from henceforth :
yea, saith the Spirit ; that they may rest from
their labours, and their works do follow them."

Lay up, O Christian people, the same kind of
consolation against that hour of terror. Wait not
to believe in death till that terrible moment breaks
up all the calm of your spirit. From this hour it
lies before you ; you have a baptism to be baptized
with ; *you must die.* Redeem the time that still
remains to you. Work the work of Him that sent
you. But, above all, remember Him who died to
conquer death for you. If we would face it un-
moved, we must not confront it alone. We must
lean on the arm of One who is stronger than we.
We must work out our own salvation with fear and
trembling, and yet be conscious that it is God that
worketh in us both to will and to do. We must
labour for God, and yet not trust at all in our own
work. For all confidence in the hour of death we
must turn to that awful cross on which our Saviour
died. He died that we might live. He suffered
that we might have courage. He cried, " Why
hast thou forsaken me ?" that we might breathe

out our souls in peace, and say, "Thou art with me, thy rod and thy staff comfort me." He said, "How am I straitened till it be accomplished," that Christians might even learn that "to live is Christ, and *to die is gain*." To believe in Christ here is to be sure of His protection in the hour of distress. Bring us safe, O Lord our Redeemer, through the terrors of the grave. Thou that art the first-fruits of our resurrection, wilt raise us up again from the dust. Thou that takest from us by death our strength of mind, our wealth, the children's faces round us, and the sweet respect of friends, thou wilt give us an hundredfold hereafter, if we trust in Thee.

> " Nothing in my hand I bring ;
> Simply to Thy cross I cling ;
> Naked, come to Thee for dress ;
> Helpless, look to Thee for grace.
>
> " While I draw this fleeting breath ;
> When my eyelids close in death ;
> When I soar to worlds unknown ;
> See Thee on thy judgment throne ;
>
> " Rock of Ages ! cleft for me,
> Let me hide myself in Thee."

III.

THE WORD OF PROPHECY.

PREACHED IN ST MARYLEBONE PARISH CHURCH, BEFORE THE LONDON SOCIETY FOR PROMOTING CHRISTIANITY AMONGST THE JEWS, MAY 4, 1865.

" We have also a more sure word of prophecy; whereunto ye do well that ye take heed, as unto a light that shineth in a dark place, until the day dawn, and the day star arise in your hearts : Knowing this first, that no prophecy of the Scripture is of any private interpretation. For the prophecy came not in old time by the will of man : but holy men of God spake as they were moved by the Holy Ghost."

THERE is much in this appeal to prophecy that is hard to be understood. If you look back for a few verses, you will perceive that it is made against those who said that Jesus Christ was not the Lord. The words might be thus paraphrased : "When we have told you that Jesus has truly come with power, and is our Christ and our Lord, we have not followed a story ingeniously devised and supported, but have only told you of a glory and a majesty which apostles have seen, and which prophets have promised." In the Asiatic Churches to which Peter wrote, grave errors had sprung up. Teachers, chiefly of Jewish origin, had denied that Jesus Christ had come in the flesh,

had denied that the facts of our Lord's humiliation would be consistent with the titles of Christ
and Lord. If He were Christ, how could He lie
in the manger, or stand in the carpenter's workshop, or be rejected and despised by despised and
rejected Nazarenes, or suffer at the hands of His
persecutors, or die on the cross, and be laid in the
tomb? Look on the records of His life, say these
false teachers; how could one who so lived and
died be the Messiah, and the glorious Son of God?
To this Peter answers by adducing two kinds of
witness. Three apostles, of whom Peter was one,
saw Christ glorified on the mount of transfiguration, and heard the *Divine* voice which out of the
splendour of the *Divine* light said, "This is my
beloved Son, in whom I am well pleased." And in
the second place, the word of prophecy bore witness
to the same Lord. "We have also," says the apostle,
"a word of prophecy, now made more sure to us
by its exact fulfilment, which was before as a
candle shining in a dark place; before the day of
Christ dawned in its brightness, and in their hearts
the day-star kindled of heaven shone that they
might see the truth. And I wish you first to bear
this in mind," he proceeds, "that no prophecy of
the *Scripture* is to be interpreted as the private

thoughts and feelings of the prophet himself. For prophecy came not of man's will, but holy men of God spake as the Holy Ghost moved them," or, as the Greek is, " bore them along."

It would be a pleasure to discuss this passage without any polemical spirit. It would be a pleasure to recall how as the wind from heaven blew stronger and stronger on the many-chorded harp of prophecy, its tones grew louder and clearer; how after the time of *D*avid it died away, and then burst forth with many voices, in the prophets whose works we possess in the Bible. But in these times of trouble the subject requires a different tone. On one side there are some amongst us who deny that the Old Testament contains, or was intended to contain, any predictions of historical facts, and who affirm that words of *S*cripture which can be shown to refer to one event, must not be so interpreted as to refer also to another; that is, they would do away all predictions and all types. On the other side, there are those of Jewish race, to whom as children of Abraham there is a birthright in the prophecies, who, feeling deeply these inspired utterances, deny that they were fulfilled in Christ. I must speak with the consciousness of both these errors, in recalling

D

to my present hearers things that they well know,
but can bear to be reminded of. In trying to show
how Old and New Testament are knit together, I
cannot of course attempt to examine passages in
detail. I shall attempt a general sketch of those
features of the New Covenant, which have thrown
forward their shadow upon the Old. If we find
that the Jewish dispensation is a *moral* system,
grounded upon the holiness of God and the danger
of sin and uncleanness; if it proposes to reconcile
the pure God and sinful man, not by the maxims
of an improved philosophy or the precepts of a
holy law, but by outward acts of sacrifice; if it
affirms, at first indistinctly, but ever with increasing clearness, that a single human agent must be
concerned in the work of redemption; if it assigns
him acts and titles that would not suit a mere king
or priest or prophet; if it attributes to him a height
of triumph and a depth of suffering which could
not meet together in the person of any human
leader, yet were found to belong to Jesus Christ;
then the Old Testament through its prophets sets
forth the same ideas as the New, and the witness
of the prophets cannot be shaken. Nor need we
for the present purpose insist on the well-known
distinction between **Law** and **Prophets**; for the

law is in a sense the prophecy, the speaking forth, by Moses the Seer, of the things that God showed him and told him to utter.

That there is in the Old Testament a looking forward to an important future for the Jewish nation, cannot be denied. In the captivity, when nothing met the eye save that which threatened national extinction and prompted to despair, the people listened to the promises of Jeremiah and Ezekiel, of a glory that yet awaited them. Their night was dark and stormy, but these their watch-men, with a sight that God had quickened, told them that the eastern sky was flushed already with the rose of dawn ; and it is remarkable that the prophets of that time of dejection speak to a suffer-ing people, not so much of a Messiah that shall suffer even as they, but rather of peace and restoration. " He that scattered Israel will gather him, and keep him as a shepherd doth his flock. For the Lord hath redeemed Jacob, and ransomed him from the hand of him that was stronger than he." (Jer. xxxi. 10, 11.) These hopes of the future, that are the characteristic of the Jewish national life, are linked almost from the first with the coming of a *person*. In the first stage of prophecy, that of the Pentateuch, the coming of Shiloh, *the man of peace*, the appearance of the prophet like unto Moses, bespeak a personal agent for the future greatness of Israel; but briefly and obscurely. In the second time, that of *David*, the word of promise is more explicit. The name of Anointed —*i.e.*, king—begins to be used. The king that shall come is to be of the lineage of *David*. He is described in His exaltation the head of a kingdom rather spiritual than temporal. And *David* dwells with grateful devotion and with no mistrust on the large promise, "I will stablish the throne of his kingdom for ever." But now words of another strain are heard mixed with these jubilant voices of hope. In the Psalms of *David* we grow accustomed to the idea of the great and good, afflicted to the death: "My God, my God, ... why hast thou forsaken me?" *David* himself, whom the Jews regarded as the type of their Messiah, was tried with sorrow and persecution. The king whom he typified should suffer the like. It was no longer strange to a Jewish mind that a king should eat the bread of affliction, and that ashes should be poured upon his purple robe. After the days of *David*, the Messianic predictions seem to cease for a time, until those prophets arose whose works are preserved in

our Bibles. They nowhere give us one full and
precise account of the Messiah that is to come;
but in many a scattered touch the picture is
gradually worked out for us. Every event that
happens to the Jews is made the occasion for
some declaration about that which God has yet
in store for them; every wind that blows sets
some string vibrating of that harp of inspiration
that broke forth into full harmony when the
angels sung to the shepherds, "Glory to God in
the highest." And the Prophets speak of Him
now as a Conqueror, or a Judge, or a Redeemer
from sin; as a Ruler of *David's* house, who
should come to restore the Jewish nation and
purify the Church. The heathen shall share the
blessing prepared for the chosen people. The
promised one is to be born in Bethlehem, of
David's line, and shall come to the second
temple; and one shall go before Him and
prepare His way. And in the 53d chapter
of Isaiah the sufferings that await Him, who
is the bearer of our griefs, the wounded for
our transgressions, are so described that we seem
to read history and not prophecy. I do not wonder that that passage has been often assailed.
It is the fortress of the Gospel; and the war must

needs gather thick about it. It is the key of the defence of the Old Testament. And so we are told that from internal evidence it is likely that it was written in the captivity, when the people had grown used to the thought of suffering. But it does so happen that in the known prophets of the captivity, Jeremiah and Ezekiel, the sufferings of Messiah are hardly mentioned ; and amidst strong rebukes for sin, God promises the renewal of His covenant with the people, and offers them pardon and peace.

With the captivity ends the third period. What were the expectations of the Jews in the fourth period, after the close of the canon of the Old Testament, we must learn chiefly from the allusions in the New. And it must be admitted that they had become earthly and material. The suffering Messiah is forgotten. They look for a king to give them once more their place among nations ; and beyond this their grovelling hopes scarcely aspire. The anointed priest and prophet, who should purify the Church of Jehovah, had passed from their minds. Here and there a Simeon discerned the sword that, smiting the shepherd, should pierce through the soul also of Mary his mother; or a John the Baptist, taught by the

Spirit of God, saw in Jesus "the Lamb of God, which taketh away the sin of the world." But the same John faltered afterwards, when the humiliation of Christ seemed too terribly real; "Art thou he that should come, or do we look for another?" Peter rebuked Jesus for announcing a fact so abhorrent to his hopes, as that the Lord must presently be betrayed, suffer, and die. And the other disciples forsook their Master, and fled the moment that a human arm was lifted against Him. After His crucifixion all hope was taken away. How could the dead redeem them? We trusted that it had been He that should have redeemed Israel. Too late we find how bitterly we were mistaken. But from the case of Simeon, and from the testimony of John the Baptist, we know that the doctrine of a suffering Messiah was not unknown at the time of our Lord, although it had receded.

Such, then, is the character of the Old Testament prophecy, through the several stages of its growth and decline. A Person, the Messiah, is associated with that future of good things for which the people was taught to look. But the fortunes of that great Prince seem to combine elements that are inconsistent. He shall sit on the throne of

*D*avid for ever; and yet die like a lamb slain for
the sins of the people. He shall reign and judge;
and yet be despised and rejected of men. He
shall subdue His enemies; yet they shall lay hands
on Him. How later Jewish teachers, pressed with
these conflicting passages, for so they seemed,
invented wild expedients to explain them, cannot
here be told: how they made two Messiahs, the
one the son of Joseph, who should die; and the
other the son of *D*avid, who should conquer: how
the Messiah was supposed to atone for sins of men,
by suffering for them before He appears in glory
on the earth. These wild dreams may have been
suggested by controversy with Christians, for they
arose in Christian times. But the point of chief
interest to us is this, that Jews who did not learn
the doctrine of suffering from the New Testament,
found passages in the Old which they confessed
to contain it, and which they could not reject,
but were forced to account for by ways of their
own.

Now it can scarcely be denied, account for it as
men may, that the New Testament takes up these
discrepant elements and reconciles them. Christ
foresees His own sufferings, and the triumph over
them. He calls Himself the victim whose blood

shall seal a new testament; but yet He does not repel the offered title of a king. From the sight of suffering inflicted on the innocent, our nature shrinks; but we can scarcely bear that the clouds of anger that have gathered over mankind for ages of guilt should discharge their fatal bolt on the head of the only sinless being that has ever borne the form of man. And yet there was a cause! The need was equal to the sacrifice! High in the secret counsels of God that need was spoken of, and the remedy found. How justice pleaded against mercy, and mercy prevailed; how sin was wiped away, whilst yet God proclaimed Himself as a hater of sin; these are mysteries about which our reason busies herself, but with small measure of success. But the heart that knows its own bitterness, appreciates the doctrine of consolation. The cross of Christ is a key that unlocks many a difficulty in the Old Testament. It has never been offered in vain to sinners that knew their sin. It was a stumbling-block to the Jews: yes, but it converted them. It was foolishness to the Greeks; but they tried to put it by, and could not. Men write essays on the rise and progress of Christianity, but they do not address themselves to the true problem. How could Christianity survive for the first days, when it preached a belief in the death and resurrection of a homeless, unlettered Galilean, unknown to most of its hearers even by name? When Peter stood up at Pentecost, and preached that Jesus, whom the Jews had crucified, and so vanquished, was Lord and Christ, why did not the preacher smile? why was not the assembly, which had shown some symptoms of a mocking spirit, dissolved in laughter? Because the word was God's eternal truth. And those whose hopes for the future had been pared down to a weak notion of some earthly resurrection that might by chance be in store for the people, had still in their hearts, though buried deep under the rubbish of frivolous and carnal memories, some traces of a better wisdom. Then flashed back upon them all the mechanism of sacrifices by which their law had uttered its daily, weekly, yearly protest against the guilt of sin. Then flashed back the solemn service of the *Day* of Atonement; and the captivity that had punished their wickedness; and the frequent descriptions of the sufferings of the good, and even of one the highest good, oppressed, imprisoned, cut off. And stirred to unusual depths, their minds discerned their own guilt, and wanted to get free from it, as a man would long for the physician, when he felt the sure symptoms of a speedy and dangerous ailment in his blood. And they saw that the man they might have deemed smitten of God, was wounded for their transgressions, bruised for their iniquities, and laden with the chastisement of their peace. They were pricked in their heart, and said, " Men and brethren, what shall we do ?"

There is indeed one difficulty for which we must be prepared, in studying the Old Testament. The predictions are drawn forth by present events, rather than uttered independently. It is full of predictions ; and yet when we examine each in its place, we find that it arose out of some present occasion ; as if a reflection on the present was the first thing, and a presage of the future only the second. Now as any form of words need not of necessity have more than one meaning, or refer to more than one event, we are asked to admit, as a canon of criticism, that no words which apply to or describe one event, are to be applied to another. This once conceded, the whole doctrine of type and prophecy is given up. But see what it amounts to. I know that in the world around me, repetition of a type is the rule, and originality the exception, if indeed the exception can be found at

all.   Through the mineral, and vegetable, and
animal kingdom, the types of crystal, and plant,
and animal are copied, varied, heightened, degraded; and, to use a common mode of speech,
nature delights to repeat herself.   What mean we
by nature ?   He who made the world, made the
men and nations on it.   We ought to be able to
know His handiwork from what we can see around
us.   When endless repetition of type with variety
in detail, is the rule in the physical world, it seems
arbitrary to insist that the events of the New
Testament cannot possibly reproduce the Old, and
that no words spoken about events in the latter
can have anything to do with the former.   If the
same great Artificer fashions the world, and also
the actions of men, we should expect to trace the
type through the one as we do through the other.

Mere human speech, indeed, limits itself to one
application just for want of foresight.   But the prophets did not utter mere human speech.   Viewing
the whole of their message, we see that they describe the future, as mere human observers could not
have done.   They were seers.   Light from on high
shone upon their minds ; now in the waking vision,
now in the dreams of sleep, now in the voice from
heaven, to which they had only to give ear.   So

they professed, and we know that their pretensions
were just, because their prophecies were pure and
holy, and have found fulfilment. Would not a
man, if he could, fashion his speech so that a present warning might embrace future dangers? When
the preacher speaks of Paul, or Pilate, or Judas,
and warns or exhorts his hearers in general terms,
would he not gladly shape his words so as to meet
the very turn and trick of their special temptation,
if he had but the light? Well, the prophet had
the light! Not always consciously, he spoke of
things to come, using things present as the theme.
If it had been said, that where words apply dis-
tinctly to one event, their second application to
another must be decided on with caution and judgment, there would have been little to object to;
for it would only express a limitation on our
powers of criticism, and not on the *D*ivine power.
But before God all things are double, one against
another. To His eye the lives and errors of nations
repeat themselves. Nations conform to their type,
as does the growing oak or the nestling bird. The
Jewish Church with its sacrificial system, its exclusion of a man from political rights until the sin
should receive its purgation with blood, was intended to resemble in those points the greater

Church, the human family, with its exclusion from
grace because of sin, and its one Great Sacrifice
by which comes restoration.   That the two should
be supposed wholly unlike, with no feature in common, is a mere arbitrary demand.   Men are the
lively stones out of which the two Churches, Jewish
and universal, are built up ; men whom the Maker
has shaped alike, down to the very fashion of a
finger-nail ; but their spiritual wants and notions
are to have no resemblance to each other.   There
is to be sacrifice in the one, and no need of it in the
other.   There is to be a painful purgation in the
one, and free forgiveness without purgation in the
other.   There is to be nothing but sacrifice in the
one, nothing but doctrine in the other.   Anger at
sin may brood over the old covenant, while the
new shall bask in the sunshine of an indiscriminate
love !   And this is reasoning !   And for the sake
of this we are to disbelieve Moses and the prophets,
and the apostles who quote them !

Did I say apostles ?   We turn to our Lord himself, in two most solemn moments of His life, and
in both of them He binds up the Old Testament
with the New.   He is supping with His disciples
for the last time.   And He will give them something by which they may recall Him and His act

of love to the end of the world. And He gives them the bread and then the cup; and with the latter He says, "*D*rink ye all of it, for this is My blood of the New Testament, which is shed for many for the remission of sins." Their thoughts went back to the days when Moses sprinkled the people with the blood of the Old Covenant, with the blood of burnt-offerings and peace-offerings, and they promised obedience to the covenant law. They saw that they were entering a new covenant, sealed with holier, more effectual blood, and making possible a higher holiness. And from that night till now the same tradition has been followed; and men have eaten the Holy Communion with special reference to the sacrifice of the death of Christ. Was that solemn charge given only to perpetuate a metaphor—and a metaphor the meaning of which would tend to be forgotten when there were no Jewish altars, no priest, no temple?

There is another moment still more solemn. The victim is lifted up upon the altar. *D*arkness covers the earth, though the sun is high. A darkness to us inscrutable clouds the spirit even of the Redeemer in that extremity of suffering, and there break from Him words, which surely at that time of all times are not permitted to escape in vain—

" My God, my God, why hast Thou forsaken me ?"
They, too, carry us back to the Old Testament.
They are the opening words of the twenty-second
Psalm. To an instructed Jew, as to us, they would
recall the whole Psalm of *David*, with its tale of
suffering, ending at last in hope and triumph. It
was a Psalm which Jewish interpreters failed not
to apply to the Messiah ; for the hopes it expresses
reach far beyond the little kingdom of the Jews.
Words which He chose to be His last, are a witness to the Old Testament ; and a claim to be the
Messiah whose sufferings stand there described.
The Old Testament had prepared us for them.
Its sin-offering, its ceremonial substitution, its
account of the Messiah, prepared us for them ;
and He ratifies the sense we had put upon the
Old Covenant, by using these momentous words
when He was consummating the New. The holy
men of old bare witness to Jesus as the coming
Son of God and Redeemer ; and Christ, in His turn,
bore witness to them that they had spoken the truth.
His last ministerial act preserved the memory of
a sacrifice for ever. His last words confirmed a
prophecy. The prophecies, we see, were of no private interpretation ; they were torches held up by
the wayside to lighten the path of Him that should

come. And I doubt not that if we set out with the belief that Christ is true, that the history of His life, as we find it, is a real history, we shall find in the Old Testament, too, the footsteps of His coming. There we shall find our sins rebuked, and read the impossibility of our restoration, save by the blood of Him who died and rose again. The blood of bulls and goats set right again in their position, as Jewish citizens, them that had sinned, and so they were forgiven. But this was an earthly forgiveness. Before the judgment-seat of Heaven it was impossible that the blood of bulls and goats should take away sin. More than a mere ceremony must take place to purge the inward clinging defilement. And thus even from the Old Testament we learn to understand the great act which made the New Covenant sure. " All we like sheep have gone astray; we have turned every one to his own way ; and the Lord hath laid on Him the iniquity of us all."

Members of the Society for Promoting Christianity amongst the Jews, the time is full of trial and anxiety. Preach to Jews the strict connexion between the Old Testament and the New, and you are met too often by a rough disbelief of the New Testament, gathered from some current books

E

Preach that Jesus is the Messiah, and you find
that the Jewish mind is preoccupied with doubts
about the earthly life of Jesus. Yet let us preach
the same doctrine, and hope for its effects. It may
be that the hour is passed by for a large ingathering of the Jews as a whole race, into the gospel
field. It may be (God knoweth) that those who
have put from them the gospel intended first of all
for them, for many ages, find the path now so
thorny with doubts, that few of them will dare
to tread it. But surely the perils of the hour
establish a community of interest between a believing Christian and a believing Jew. Both are occupied now in one task, in defending the historical
and prophetical books of the Old Testament from
attack. They must needs, when they fight side
by side, compare each other's weapons. The Jew
will be forced to revise with care the ideas which
his treasured Bible gives him; and this is the
Christian's opportunity for showing that those
ideas are crowned and completed in Christ, and
that the Bible without the New Testament is but
half a book, whilst both are the Word and Wisdom of God. And even out of the scepticism
about the life of Jesus, which has unquestionably
prepossessed many Jews against us, good may be

elicited. If France gives us for the inspired Gospels a historical romance, and Germany offers to prove that there are no historical materials on which to found it, then when the false witnesses agree not together against the Lord, let us be instant with our New Testament in our hands, in begging the hearers who are to judge, to search our Scriptures for themselves. They will know Christ, they will love Him. There will come upon them the feeling that He is a witness whom they could accept. And He witnesses to the intimate connexion of the Old and New. Yes, the gospel of the kingdom, now a great and strong tree, strikes its roots downwards through the strata of many Jewish ages. Abraham and Moses, and Isaiah and John the Baptist have their share in the message, as Peter, John, and Paul have theirs. Those are the roots; these are the branches. We fear nothing from reverent study. What, indeed, can come from it but a fuller perception of the deep harmonies which law and gospel breathe? What but greater knowledge of the character, and wisdom, and ineffable love of Jesus, which will draw men unto Him, as they have ever done. Oh! those prodigal children for whom the best seat and the richest robe were once prepared, and in whose place of favour we are sitting through their default. Our hearts yearn towards them. Buried through centuries in Gentile slough and slime, the marks of a people are still upon them. Those whom God chose once we can still find in every land, and the image and superscription still are there.

Poor wanderers from their God! Hark to the distant sound of their imprecation—" His blood be upon us, and on our children." Are they thus marked by God's justice—His vengeance? Nay, we are Christ's; we make no discourse of vengeance, but of love. We, like them, have done all too much to bring His blood upon us by our guilt. Go out into the highways and hedges, and compel them to come in.

IV.

PEACE AND WAR.

*PREACHED TO THE NATIONAL RIFLE ASSOCIATION AT
WIMBLEDON, JULY 17, 1864.*

" So there went one on horseback to meet him, and said, Thus
saith the king, Is it peace ? And Jehu said, What hast thou
to do with peace? turn thee behind me. And the watchman
told, saying, The messenger came to them, but he cometh not
again."

THE history whence these words are taken is
easy to recall. No more vivid description is
found in the Holy Book. Jehu, the brave and ruth-
less captain of the host at the siege of Ramoth Gilead,
is suddenly accosted by a strange messenger, who
demands an interview. When they are alone the
visitor produces a vessel of the holy oil and pours
it over the head of Jehu, and after this unction
salutes him as King of Israel, raised up to avenge
the wickedness of the house of Ahab. Than the
fierce and vehement Jehu no fitter instrument of
vengeance could have been found. Ere any alarm
could be given to those who were in Jezreel, the
watchman on its walls saw the cloud of dust that
marked the approach of Jehu, driving in madness, as the Hebrew phrase describes him. Was it

peace or war ?   It was extermination for the
house of Ahab, by cruelty and stratagem.   The
work of retribution was thoroughly performed.
He slew Jehoram and cast his body into the field
of Naboth.   Jezebel met the death she had so
well deserved.   Ahab's seventy sons were slain
by his orders.   All the heathen population of
Israel were massacred at once, when Jehu pre-
tended to offer with them the sacrifice to Baal.
Jehu reigned long after this, and his house was
established and lasted longer than any other
dynasty in Israel.   But in all this graphic account, what strikes us most and moves the deepest
thoughts in us, is, that the young man who anointed
this cruel, crafty, and furious instrument was a messenger from Elisha the prophet of God ; and so the
work of destruction was cast upon him by the command of God.

Centuries pass, and the reign of Jehu, which had
never, in spite of all the warrior's vehemence and
zeal, produced any solid good to his nation, has
become almost forgotten.   In the solemn phrase
of the sacred historian, " Jehu slept with his
fathers."   And from the land where he lived,
where he sleeps, all royal glory has faded, and a
reduced and humbled people feed their pride upon

the memory of the past, and upon hopes held out
to them of a new prince who shall recreate the
national greatness. Not far from Esdraelon, where
once the watchman had seen the destroyer swoop-
ing with the haste of madness upon the prey that
had been given over to him, there was reared in
Nazareth a conqueror of another temper, a messenger from God of another spirit. Jesus, like the
fiery Jehu, had His work and His divine commission. He came to the same people to rule them ;
He moved upon the same scenes, but in all else
how different! In the spirit of peace that breathed
from Him, in the reception that His people ac-
corded Him, in the grand purpose that moved His
whole life, in the fate that He encountered, the
Saviour of the world was as different as could
be from the destroyer of those that killed the
prophets. Jehu greeted the name of peace with
savage mockery, "What hast thou to do with
peace?" Peace was the watchword of the Redeemer's ministry. The angels sang over His
cradle, "Peace on earth." After the bitterness of
death was past the risen Saviour said, "Peace be
unto you." If the blood of prophets was to be
visited so heavily on Ahab's seed, how much sorer
might have been the punishment of them who

dragged the Lord of prophets to the foot of the cross? But He called forth no avenging legions to scatter them that mocked Him, that scourged Him, that lied against Him. Love, and peace, and mercy, offered to all alike, these were the gifts He came to bring. And how were His gifts received? Jehu reigned long over the people that he awed to submission. Jesus came to His own! and His own received Him not; He offered them life and blessing, and they cursed Him and condemned Him to die; they chose a thief before Him, they took on themselves and their children the guilt of His blood. And yet the one came but to destroy the enemies of God. The other came to work the grandest and most far-seeing reformation that was ever known to mankind.

Now these two dispensations, the dispensation of justice and the dispensation of love, so opposite in all points, did in fact proceed from one and the same divine will. The sword of Jehu and the healing voice of Christ had, in fact, this common origin; they were both part of the divine economy for the conquest over evil. One of them flashed forth in vengeance and retribution, the other breathed love even to the most unworthy. But both alike were in this point divine, that they

marked the enormity of sin in the sight of God;
albeit, the one consumed the sinner and his house,
and the other lifted up the sinner and bid him go
free, because One who had done no sin was ready
to suffer in his stead. It is permitted us to say
that the spirit of the gospel is a higher spirit than
that severe exactness in punishment which the Old
Testament exhibits; for our Lord himself and
His apostles tell us that the gospel is higher than
the law. We do not thereby pretend that the
Omnipotent knew not the effect of His own counsels, and, like some unpractised artificer, having
tried one mode of working and having found it
fail, cast it aside to make a fresh experiment. We
do not charge God with imperfection. But, for
some mysterious reason, which we cannot measure,
which we need not measure if we could, the disease
of man's waywardness was not yet rife for its
appropriate and sufficient medicine. And all the
dealings of JEHOVAH in the old dispensation, all
those portents in the desert, that pilgrimage of
forty years, those strict and minute laws, those
judges and kings and fervid prophets fearless in
rebuke, those chapters of the history of vengeance
and punishment, whereof the very pages seem
•sickly with the odour of carnage, those acts of

making over into the power of her enemies the chosen people of the Most High, all these are so many expedients and palliatives to modify the course of the great plague of sin, until the hour shall arrive when the Physician shall come in, and prescribe the true and only remedy, bidding the sick sufferer "deny himself and take his cross and follow Him."

These things we can fully understand; we are willing to admit them. But now comes our great perplexity. The more perfect and excellent way has not yet prevailed over the less excellent. Our gathering here to-day is a proof of it. We are assembled to learn the gospel of peace, to own the guilt of our sins, to taste the sweet savour of forgiveness, to praise the Lord of heaven and earth. Yesterday the sharp crack of many a rifle was answered by the ringing proof that the aim had been true, and that if need were the life of a man was in that marksman's power. We belonged on Saturday to a world of strife; on Sunday we bow down before the Prince of Peace. How can these things be? How justify this old warfare and reign of force and terror eighteen hundred years after that new law was given, " I say unto you that ye resist not evil: but whosoever shall·

smite thee on thy right cheek, turn to him the other also. And if any man will sue thee at the law, and take away thy coat, let him have thy cloke also. And whosoever shall compel thee to go a mile, go with him twain." What can it profit that men praise us for patriotism, and tell us that our skill has made our country safe from foreign aggression, if our existence is a contradiction to the gospel that we profess?

Brethren, the new law of the gospel, so full of love, so profound, so ennobling in its observance, may begin at once to do its work in the heart, as soon as its divine prescriptions are understood. You can at once learn to forgive the personal wrong, to chasten and purify from uncleanness the thoughts of your heart, to be truthful in speech, to submit to evil where the loss falls only upon you, to love even them that hate you. Blessed indeed are we if we have thus recognised at once its divine obligations, and suffered it, or rather suffered Him that spake it, to fashion us anew unto holiness. For there will be a life hereafter, and a polity in heaven, where no other law shall prevail; and it is well for us if we are training ourselves for that citizenship of the heavenly Jeru-salem. But when we look round us and find a

world full of resistance to that law, we understand
that the very fact that it *is* resisted, limits us, too,
in our adoption of it as a rule. What! shall I
refuse to swear in a court of justice, because He
said, *S*wear not at all, when there are many who
will only yield up a true witness under the pressure of an oath? Then I shall help them to escape
speaking the truth, and so the cause of truth would
suffer, and the very purpose of the precept, which
is that men may speak the simple truth, would be
made of no effect. What! when some invader
attempts to violate our coasts, will that be the
time to preach that ye resist not evil? Again,
the very purpose of the precept would be frus-
trated. *S*hall our country be subdued, and with
its humiliation shall free institutions be endan-
gered throughout the world? *S*hall the blessings
of equal laws and of pure scriptural teaching, be
risked and perhaps swept away? I may be willing for myself to offer my cheek to the smiter, but
I have no right by preaching non-resistance to
bring evil upon my fellow-countrymen, upon
millions of the same blood and race and language.
And so, whilst we admit that the new law is the
highest and most binding, we must see at the
same time that there are limits to its present appli-

cation. To keep it, to treasure it up in our heart of hearts, should be the aspiration of all Christian men. But the world has much resisted it, and there are evils and oppressions still which seem to require the stern interference of some captain of the host to punish them. He who has tried the most to practise in and for himself the beautiful self-denial of the gospel, will still feel his pulse throb and his cheek tingle at the story of a stronger nation pressing a weaker one to its destruction. When the invader in his cruel selfishness breaks through the silken cords of the gospel, and seems to know no law but that of selfishness, it seems that stern language would alone be understood. "What hast thou to do with peace? Turn thee behind me."

Volunteers, the institution which you represent is lawful. It was a necessity even under the gospel for our safety, perhaps for our existence. It never can become the instrument of oppression, or the nursery of cruelty, or the temptation to a career of conquest. There ran a whisper round amongst us that our land might be coerced by an invasion, and ere our scattered fleets could turn their wings homeward over the sea, a great blow might be struck at the free institutions, of which we have long been the pattern and repository, at our religion, at our commerce. It was no wrong impulse, be sure of it, that made all classes of the community start up to refute this whisper of alarm. "What God has given us, that we will keep safe for ourselves and our children." Had the attempt been made our chalky cliffs would have been topped by a living rampart such as an invader would hardly seek to encounter. There has been peace therefore, and the thought of invasion has died away. And this generous outburst of patriotism was no passing emotion. It has organised an army, the flower of which is gathered round us to-day from every district in this island ; an army serving for no reward, and acquiring steadily year by year, without the stimulus of actual war, a unique skill in the use of its chosen weapon. There is nothing inconsistent with the need of love that you have resolved, that behind your iron hedge the men and women and children of England shall sleep secure. And with this indispensable sense of safety other advantages have come. You have made manly ways, and a manly submission to discipline, and contempt for softness and luxury, popular in all classes. You have snatched up the small and unconsidered fragments of time, which before you might have thought it permissible to waste, and have made yourselves skilled soldiers in them. But just because so much has been done, let me plead for something more. The influence of this one idea has been felt throughout all classes. You possess a power which every corner of the nation feels, and that for good. And if we were living in the times of the Sauls and Jehus, it were enough that the work of God were done faithfully; and the thoughts and temper of the doer would have been tested only by his faithfulness in the particular task assigned him. Saul was rejected because he faltered in obedience; Jehu was established on his throne because he did his work thoroughly, although his work was the merciless destruction of the wicked and his seed. Christians cannot so be judged, whether they are soldiers, or citizens, or ministers of God. The law of Christ reaches down to the thoughts, the heart, the spirit of man. For rough-handed soldiers, driving in their recklessness to new scenes of blood, the gospel has no place. War is a remnant of the old and harsher covenant, which must endure into the covenant of love, simply because of the evil tempers of mankind that are still unsubdued; and because the law of Christ cannot have its perfect

F

operation except where it is leavening *the whole
mass.* But you are soldiers of Christ as well as
soldiers of your Queen. At your baptism the cross
was marked upon you, in token that hereafter you
should not be ashamed to confess the faith of Him
crucified, and manfully to fight under His banner
against sin, the world, and the devil, and continue
His faithful soldiers and servants unto your lives'
end. You have in hand a work for your Lord as
well as a work for your country.

What is that work? My friends, it lies in the
social influence you possess. I suppose that a
more sudden and powerful change has never been
witnessed than you have helped to make in the
habits of our young men, of that class which we
ministers find it so difficult to reach, because of its
occupations, its passions, its self-confidence; you
belong to it for the most part; you influence it
through and through. See what beautiful order
and precision has been suddenly brought to bear
upon these annual contests; not enforced upon you
by martial law, but the spontaneous outgrowth
of your own good will and sense of order. Oh
that these qualities may have their highest application! Oh that such a power may be turned into
the service of the Lord Christ! Oh that we may

be encouraged, from the very suddenness and
completeness of this movement, to believe that
men can be moved and stirred even to higher
uses, can be turned from darkness to light, from
the power of Satan unto God! There must be
many that hear me whose minds are already earnestly desirous to serve the cause of Christ. To
these, I say, Your work lies here before you ; you
have to raise the tone of this movement, and ever
more and more to raise it, so that that which on
its outward face is a bulwark against the foreign
foe, shall from its inner surface reflect the light of
Christ upon our young men, and remind them
what a Christian soldier should be. You have
already conquered laziness and lounging habits ;
you have emptied haunts of dissipation ; let that
encourage you to higher successes. Yes, we will
fashion our lives in holiness so as to be able to say
to our brethren with the apostle, " Be followers of
me, as I am of Christ." We will make our healthy
examples felt through all the pulses of our national
life, for purity of conduct, for sobriety, for piety,
for love of our brethren. We will see that there is
never laid to the charge of this great movement
the wrong of any woman; the ruin of any home
through the dissipation of its head, the prevalence

of any vice of speech or act. We will associate
with this movement a strain of Christian chivalry
of its own, of which purity and piety and unselfish-
ness shall be the tokens. We will have nothing
enter into it that may lower and defile it. Then,
great as is the political significance of this assembly,
the religious influence of it would be greater still.
The storms of war are stirring through all the
atmosphere; they have not reached us, perhaps
because we are prepared, but this is not an army
of Jehu the son of Nimshi, that has no work except
amidst destruction. We are soldiers of Christ;
and His war is ever being carried on. It is a war
against sin and evil, in us, in those around us.
He will fight for us; He will ever find us service
to do. Our arms will never rust in inaction. May
we indeed be His soldiers and servants, and find
in that our happiness and our reward.

V

"I WILL GIVE YOU REST."

PREACHED IN YORK MINSTER TO A CONGREGATION OF WORKING MEN, JANUARY 13, 1867.

"Come unto me, all ye that labour and are heavy laden, and I will give you rest. Take my yoke upon you, and learn of me; for I am meek and lowly in heart: and ye shall find rest for your souls. For my yoke, is easy and my burden is light."

CHRIST promises to be the rest of souls! Consider this well. No man ever made a greater claim. It were a small thing in comparison to promise to possess and govern all the kingdoms of the world. We have seen something like that within a century. It is almost a hundred years since a man was born in a small island who became ruler of the French people, and kept the world in awe of his name. Long afterwards the power of that name supplanted a dynasty, and placed a kinsman on the throne. But who can give rest for souls? Who dares pretend to it? The doctor that can give rest to the body refuses to "minister to the mind diseased;" it is too deep to reach: "Herein the patient must minister to

himself," says the poet.　But here is one who
claims this power—" I will give you rest "—a
power beyond the power of kings, a wisdom beyond the reach even of our science; a power and
wisdom which prove the claimant to be divine, if
the claim is true; to be the vainest pretender, if it
is false.

And it is true.　Christ is and has been the giver
of rest.　Even those who have not come very close
to religion, even those who think it only a senti-
ment with which some people delude themselves,
own that it is a resource and a repose to them in
sorrows and troubles.　Death smites; and the
survivors say, "It is the Lord! let Him do what
seemeth Him good," and they are comforted by
saying it.　Sickness confines them to a tedious
bed; and they say, " We suffer; but He suffered
more," and they smile at the tedium of their sickness; and you may visit them after ten or fifteen
weary years of sickness, and find them smiling
still.　Oh! that the thought of Christ does bring
with it a certain sweet peace and consolation, not
a delusion but a real thing, because it prevails over
sufferings that are painfully real, cannot well be
denied.

Looking closer at His own well-known words to-

night, we will try to see what our Lord promises
for our souls, what He does for them.

' I. Now first, He offers them rest from the law of
Moses. This we know from the expression, "Take
my *yoke* upon you." To speak of the yoke of the
law was so far common among Jews, both learned
and simple, that. the hearers would understand at
once what this verse meant. I have a new law to
give you, and when compared with the old law it
is easy and light. Notice again this quiet claim
to divine power. The old law came from God; it
is "holy and just and good." But here is a promise of a better, and from a man. Who is this who
will improve and alter even God's own law?

The new law is better than the old. You may
compare these two laws or covenants in this way.
Think first of a city which has been the scene of
great outbreaks and tumults, so that soldiers are
sent there, and martial law proclaimed, and the
very first token of disaffection is most severely
punished. Men are not allowed to wear certain
colours in their dress, nor to play the tunes of
certain songs, nor to be abroad late at night; because suspicion attaches to all these things. Such
a condition is a hard one, and yet a useful and

beneficent one. It is hard, because it is full of suspicion and repression, and because its rules are vexatious and its punishments prompt and inexorable. But it is useful too, because the worst evil in a city is disorder, and that is checked, and the well-disposed can pursue their callings, and rapine and murder dare not show their face. Now that is like the Mosaic law. It is a sore burden, in one point of view, because its rules are many and troublesome, so that no man can keep them all; and they are checks to our free action, and we would rather be free from them altogether. But the law was also holy and good; yes, precious beyond all precious things that God had yet given His creatures; because it showed that over our tumultuous race there was still a living Jehovah, and that He hated disorder, which is sin, and would not suffer it to endure. It did not make the Jews holy, or well-affected towards their great King. But it did wonders for them in that respect, when you set them beside other nations. Others hewed idols out of every tree and every quarry; and studied sensual wickedness with an abstruse and hideous ingenuity. Amongst the Jews was ever present a true, and a prevailing, witness for the one God, and against the sins which

He abhorred; and they were saved thereby from idolatry and from infinite excess. But now imagine that in that city, with its silent streets and watchful sentries, there is a happy home, where a kind and wise father governs his children by the mere force of love. None of them wishes to conceal a thought from their father; they have no fear of him; they ask his advice in all things; they love the room where he sits; they are ashamed when they have done anything that brings a look of pain into his face. In that house, though there reigns far more peace than in the city without, no one thinks that there is any law. Love is the life of that happy dwelling: love is its light; love has driven out of it corruption of morals and slavish fear. It wants no other law. That house, my friends, is an image of the kingdom of God. The law did much in preventing crime and idolatry. But to earnest souls there was an incurable void in it. The more they looked into and saw God's perfection, the more did they feel their own misery and deformity. It was like a poor ragged leper, with his scales and blotches, standing in the doorway of a banqueting hall, and seeing all the fair and splendid apparel, all the noble and beautiful guests, and shrinking back miserable into the outside darkness, knowing that if he entered all would fall back in terror and disgust from him. The earnest man would say, "The law bids me to all that is good—would raise me to great heights of goodness, if I could love it and observe it. Unhappily, I cannot love it, and so fail to observe it." "Oh wretched man that I am!" (these are St Paul's words on the subject,) "who shall deliver me from the body of this death?" St Paul knew the answer; he only asks the question on purpose to answer it. The Lord had told him. "Come unto me, all ye that labour and are heavy laden." Come unto me, that is, you in whom conscience has begun to work and struggle, and to try to deliver herself from the load of sin that sits on her bowed neck. "I will give you rest." I give you comfort in feeling that even sin is not too great for me to deal with. They should know Him as the divine Son, and yet their friend. They should feel that He had taken them by the hand, and admitted them to all the love and the peace of the family of God. Jews brought near their divine Lawgiver shook with terror. "If we hear the voice of the Lord God any more we shall die." Christians, full of affection for their Lord, cling to Him in their trouble, and say, "Lord, to whom shall we go? Thou hast the words of eternal life."

Oh blessed revelation of the gospel, the forgiveness of sins! What to me is all the rest of the creed without that article? Tell me that God is holy, is eternal, is the Lord of me and mine; I will believe you. I will adore Him as all these. But the more I think on these attributes, the clearer do I see how far above me this glorious Lord hath set Himself. The man of science tells us that the stars, that like ten thousand diamond sparks adorn the robe of heaven, are every one of them suns, some far brighter than our own, whose distances cannot be written down, because one page is too narrow for the millions on millions, be the unit as large as you will. I wonder; but they are far and high, not made for me, never to be known by me. So towards the Maker of them all I look with wonder; but if my sin has set a distance between me and Him, which neither tears of mine nor costly sacrifices can abridge, I can only wonder and fear. A voice says, "Thy sins be forgiven thee. Peace with God has been procured for thee by the life and death of Jesus. Look up to God as thy Father, reconciled to His lost son." All is changed by this message. God seemed too great

to think of us, and our maimed and ruined plight.
Now, we see He is too great to lose sight of anything.　Meek and lowly in heart, the Saviour, who
was present at creation, when all those splendours
were poured forth, and knows their names and
number, descends to earth, and gathers out His
sheep, tends them, feeds them, carries them in His
arms.　The troubled mind learns of Him forgiveness and rest.

II. Christ gives rest from worldly trouble.　Care
and sorrow are confined to no class ; and whilst
the troubles of the poor are the hardest, every one
of whatever grade has sometimes felt the need of
rest from trials that have threatened to become
intolerable.　And what is rest in this sense ?
Something sure, for us to return to and repose
on, when we have found the promises of hope
deceitful.　Something that may be balm of love
to our wounded heart when a friend plays us false,
or men put an evil meaning on our best intentions,
or return kind efforts with hatred.　Something
which may remind us of the love of God when
the hard laws of nature which He has appointed
seem to threaten our destruction.　We all crave
alike, in the trying incidents of life, for words of

sympathy, for a finger to point out new objects of hope beyond the present distress, for the presence of a friend whom we can thoroughly know and trust. The friend we all desire is one who has wisdom, sympathy, and strength. To whom shall we go? Christ is ready; and all these, and more than these, are His. The Christ that once was visible, soothing ruffled tempers among His disciples, subduing paltry ambitions, bearing with a dulness that was more of heart than of head, always standing between men and the inexorable death itself, a new witness to God's mercy among them, who had too much cause to feel His power, Christ has proved already that He can give rest. And men turn to the Rock of Ages when they find they have not faith to walk on the restless sea of their life, for they know that the Rock is strong and sure. Those that have little trouble do not know how much of this ministry of comfort our dear Lord is still discharging amongst us. Lately I went to visit the scene of that great calamity which has called forth so much sympathy,* in order to say a word of comfort, albeit I knew how powerless words must seem under the pressure of a great affliction. But One had been there

* The Oaks Colliery.

already, whose words do not fail. Much of the sorrow was mixed with resignation. It was not the cry of despair that could see nothing in the affliction but sheer loss, nothing but the natural outcome of certain laws neglected. I found in many cases of utter, and, in one sense, hopeless bereavement, a feeling after resignation, an endeavour of the heart to utter words which are the hardest of all to speak: "It is the Lord! let Him do what seemeth Him good." Christ was there, preparing rest for them that were so heavy laden. He was doing there that greatest of His works, teaching wisdom out of trouble, conquering the evils of this life by whispering peace to the sufferer.

Whenever any soul learns to see and love God's hand in affliction, there Christ is the teacher. Who first taught men the use of sorrow? Jesus, who through sorrow saved us. Who first taught men the dignity of sorrow? The same *Saviour*, by going amongst the sorrowful, and weeping with them and consoling them.

> " He is my God,
>   Though dark my road ;
> He holds me that I shall not fall,
> Wherefore to Him I leave it all."

Those who can feel that truth are very nigh to

Christ. They could have learnt it from no other master.

And this is the reason that we call any great and striking affliction a visitation of God. We must not confound visitation with judgment, or with punishment. A visitation means a more solemn visit. Once at least in the New Testament it has a kind and good sense. "Because thou knewest not the time of thy visitation," means "Because thou knewest not the time when the Lord would visit thee in mercy." Why do you call a mere explosion of a collection of gases, brought about by fixed laws of nature, a visitation? Because Christ does visit His people at such times, and quickens and improves their moral state by the very means which inflict such ruin on their homes and means of living. The Lord is called the Shepherd and Bishop of our souls ; and in the Greek the word bishop means visitor. The two words are of the same root, bishop and visitation, (*episcopos, episcope,*) the provident inspector and the inspection. By the word visitation we only state a fact. Those that are Christ's own people are then most conscious of His presence when their need of Him is greatest. You on whom life's trials press hardest, you who stand nearest to

G

the brink of any public trouble, because your own
and your children's bread are in jeopardy, to you
Christ speaks, " I will give you rest." The yoke
of your lot galls you ; its burden bears you down.
You wish to die from sheer weariness of an over-
tasked soul. Christ will make even your yoke
easy, and your burden light. Your trouble, which,
apart from religion, might be traced to some other
source—accident call it, or laws of nature, or state
of labour-market, or whatever it be—is used as
the occasion of a visit from the Bishop of your
souls. Then when trouble has broken up and
pulverised the hard soil of your heart, His hand is
ready with the seed to sow therein. Without this,
accidents and disease and distress would seem a
kind of warfare between man and the powers of
nature, in which the powers of nature always prove
too strong for us. Christ tells us these strokes
are not all evil. The hard stone that hurts the
foot we dash against it is full of golden grains.
Christ teaches us how a blow may become a treasure. None but Christians can be content with
sorrow. Even they find it hard ; but they learn it
at last.

> " I do not ask, O Lord, that life may be
> A pleasant road

I do not ask that Thou wouldst take from me
    Aught of its load ;
I do not ask that flowers should always spring
    Beneath my feet,
I know too well the poison and the sting
    Of things too sweet.
For one thing only, Lord, dear Lord, I plead—
    Lead me aright,
Though strength should falter and though heart
    should bleed,
    Through peace to light." *

III. Rest for the conscience from sin, rest for the mind and body from trouble, such are the Lord's beneficent gifts to us. I might speak, if time permitted, of another rest—rest in the hour of death. "Are not my days few?" said Job, unsettled by his affliction ; "cease then, and let me alone, that I may take comfort a little, before I go whence I shall not return, even to the land of darkness and the shadow of death ; a land of darkness as darkness itself ; and of the shadow of death, without any order, and where the light is as darkness." But one who has already known Jesus as the justifier of the ungodly and the consoler of his wretchedness, one who has put his hand trustingly into that of his Lord to lead him through these perils, will not shrink back when the path in which the Lord is leading him begins to be dark-

* A. A. Procter in Baynes' English Lyrics.

ened with the shadow of death. All will go. The estate you made; the children that want your guidance; the wife who in your death will lose more than half her being. Joys, solaces, studies, possessions, all will be exchanged for a new and unknown state. I am come to the brink of that grave; what wonder if I shrink back from the blackness of its darkness? What wonder if all past affections and employments are gilded with a sunset glow, and look brighter in contrast with the darkness that must be? It is dark, but my hand is in His, and it draws me now as I have been used to be drawn. Awful shapes surround me. Questions about the near future beset the mind. Thought and strength and courage flag in the wasting of the frame. Still He leads me on, He who has been teaching me all along that God means to do me good, and not to destroy. " Yea, though I walk through the valley of the shadow of death, I will fear no evil : for Thou art with me ; Thy rod and Thy staff they comfort me."

Rest from sin, rest from trouble, rest in death. Do you want these? We want them, all of us. But He says, " Come unto me." No apostle thus summons all men to him. He has a right greater

than apostles; He is God. Do not stand doubt-
ing whether you are of the proper stuff out of
which a religious man can ever be made. When
God says, " Come," that means that you *can* come.
Come, then, and learn of Him. Learn to put
sin away from you, and to follow the example of
Him—meek as He is, and lowly of heart. Look
for Him in everything; never act without Him.
You have your trials, and your faults; you think
it will be hard for you to live piously. Well;
your Master shows that He is divine, by doing
what is hard. Children of sin and sorrow, why
will ye die, under the very shadow of the great
Rock, from which the fountains of sweet water are
ready to break forth for your refreshment? Come,
by wishing to know Christ better. Come, by
praying to Him to take charge of your poor foolish wasting life. Come, by looking on your sins
with shame. Come, by believing Him to be the
way, the truth, and the life. Come, by stretching
out a willing hand to that great Friend, strong as
God and loving as He is strong. He is yours,
though you have to labour for bread, and often to
want it. Your right in Christ is measured by your
need, and nothing else. Come to Him, you that

struggle and are overburdened in the struggle. Ask His help; bid Him take you wholly, and lead you through storm and dim twilight and deep night of sorrow, to the perfect day—to the rest prepared for the people of God.

VI.

REVERENCE FOR CHILDREN.

*PREACHED AT WESTMINSTER ABBEY, BEFORE THE
NATIONAL SOCIETY,* 1863.

"And it came to pass, that after three days they found Him in the temple, sitting in the midst of the doctors, both hearing them, and asking them questions. And all that heard Him were astonished at His understanding and answers. And when they saw Him, they were amazed : and His mother said unto Him, Son, why hast Thou thus dealt with us? behold, Thy father and I have sought Thee sorrowing. And He said unto them, How is it that ye sought me? wist ye not that I must be about my Father's business? And they understood not the saying which He spake unto them."

ONLY in this little story, preserved by one evangelist, are we suffered to catch a glimpse of the childhood of Jesus. And often, perhaps, we have passed it over as a mere prelude to the history, interesting indeed, but well-nigh needless, as delaying, rather than helping, the account of a great conflict, of a great life and a cruel death, pregnant with interest to us and to the world. Yet I will venture to say that not one page in the Bible is more full of instruction. Between the glorious rising of the Sun of Righteousness in the birth of

Jesus, and the noonday shining of that Sun when Jesus, at the age of thirty, wrought wonders and taught the people, a cloud veils Him for the most part from our sight. At this point only is it lifted, and the light falls upon a group the most remarkable: upon doctors of the law teaching to a child of twelve their views of Jehovah's ways and Jehovah's law; upon the parents, puzzled first at the loss of their child, and then at the solemn answer, almost of rebuke, with which He met their expostulations; and, lastly, upon the central figure, that Child Himself, who had wandered from the side of His parents, not for toys or pleasures or waywardness, but seeking light because He was Light; hearing and questioning about the way of salvation, and the truth of revelation, and the life of righteousness, because He is the Way and the Truth and the Life. And many wonders attach to that group: the scribes are teaching One who should teach them; the mother of Jesus rebukes her son for engaging in that which was the very business which He came to fulfil. And Jesus condescends to be taught of man! That perfect wisdom, that sinlessness of life, that break forth upon us in His manhood, grew, and were trained through childhood and youth; and the Lord's example, which has consecrated for us the infant's cradle, the temptation, the sorrow and death to which we all are subject, has consecrated for us education also. He submitted to those whose teaching He would afterwards overthrow; and He who in manhood found His Father's business in declaring with authority His Father's will, found it now in sitting meekly at the feet of appointed teachers. He has approved obedience to authority in His youth, as He has done self-sacrifice and love for souls in His manhood.

But out of all this scene one would select for its human interest the attitude of the mother of Jesus for an instruction to ourselves. There has descended into her humble home a treasure too great for heaven itself to contain. There has been given to her for guidance, training, even for ad-monition and reproof, One whose words will be the law of the earth; One to whom she herself must be beholden for everlasting redemption. What wonder if she fails to understand the value of this divine Son—if she wholly mistakes the meaning of His absence, which has caused her such concern? What wonder if she applies to the case the com-monplace rebuke, " Thy father and I have sought Thee sorrowing"? Nay, but we may be told it

was inexcusable in one who remembered the marvels of His birth, and all that then occurred, to
chide Him for resorting to the Temple, and to be
astonished that He sat with doctors and heard and
questioned them. Twelve years of meek obedience
in common household tasks and duties had passed
since His birth. Miracles, which are meant to
witness to doctrines, were not, we may be sure,
performed to startle the carpenter's humble family;
and she had forgotten in some measure the significant tokens of the past, and the dutiful boy was to
her the future carpenter, the support of her age,
the inmate of her house, or of some frugal house
like hers to the end, and the air of authority sat
easy upon her, for her right had not been disputed.

But other rights asserted themselves now. The
light within Him breaks out now from behind
the veil of flesh. " How is it that ye sought me?
wist ye not that I must be about my Father's
business?" Other claims and other ties super-
sede, or soon shall do so, the calm family life.
He shall dwell with that Father who in His Baptism, His transfiguration, His death, will attest
that this One is the Son of God. He shall seek
for brethren and for children in all whom the ties
of a common faith in His Father unite to Him.

His work shall not be with the axe and hammer in Joseph's workshop, but it shall lie in turning souls from darkness to light, from death to life, from the power of Satan unto God. What wonder if the mother after the flesh cannot at once train her ear to the full compass of this new revelation? Where is the inconsistency in her believing that the son should be subject to her still, whose birth was promised by angels, heralded by miracles, attested by the outpouring of prophecies? Twelve years of obedience, of gentleness, of love, had been vouchsafed to her, and these were her assurance for the future. What mother would wish them broken up? A sword shall pierce through her own soul also ; but what mother would plant the point of it against her own heart? Her thoughts ran naturally in the channel of a calm domestic relation with her son, of a life not indeed without hardness and trial, but sweetened by affectionate union. She will acquiesce, but not till she has painfully learned the plan of God, in the life of battle, with all forms of evil, which He shall lead in the face of Satan and his host, where she is not, where she shall be met, if she venture into its sphere, by words of strangeness—" Woman, what have I to do with thee?" Some have entertained angels

unawares; but the King whom angels serve is a
sojourner under her roof; she has to unlearn the
speech of a mother, and learn that of a worshipper
of the adorable Son of God and her Redeemer.
She must cease to command and to admonish,
and kneel with the rest of us before the Cross that
was reared for all our guilty race alike.

All mothers may look with interest on this perplexity, for they may well have felt something of
it themselves. Children are born to us, and we
clasp them to our heart as a gift of God sent here
to lend fresh motives to our life, and to soften it
with fresh joys. Whatever they say or do we
treasure, and admire beyond its worth. Before
they have done anything to earn our love, we have
trusted them in advance with all the love our
hearts can give. We cannot render a reason for
the dear regard in which we hold them. We refuse to our greatest benefactors such love as we
lavish upon these helpless, immature beings, dependent on us at every stage of their life. The
love is without stint; the right over them seems
complete; the bond between us seems perpetual.
Not so: this child also is to be reared as a child of
God. He, too, has a Father in heaven, and soon
he begins to lisp of things eternal, and to ask

questions about that other world, and death, and God, and the state hereafter, which remind us that he, too, must be about his Father's business. And then the love is changed to reverence : a child is not the darling of our home and the toy of our leisure, but a precious trust from God to us, capable of rendering service to God here, nay, bound so to render it. And we are bound to equip it for that service, and to teach it to aim at higher love than ours, at better approbation, at more complete reward. Our affections sublimed by the thought that God, and not we, is the Father whom our child should reverence, will learn to desire that our child's face should turn upwards, past our own, to the Father that is throned in heaven. We shall persuade ourselves to long that in that young mind we may decrease, if so God may increase. We shall teach it not to bound its hopes by the pleasures or comforts we can procure for it; but to seek peace from above. Nay : we shall learn not to sorrow as men without hope, if death should lay a cold hand upon that curled head and radiant brow. The Father who gave may take back. What matters it if our hearth be desolate, if our house echoes to no childish laughter, if the object of our love is compassed in the embrace of a better love, and taken to a home of enduring peace? Words hard to speak, and yet felt by us to be true. For children are a precious trust; they are not mere jewels and ornaments to deck out our success, but souls sent here by God to us to be trained and reared for Him. We understand the change that opened before Mary, the mother of many sorrows, when those words were uttered, "How is it that ye sought me?" God has sought and claimed thy son. Love him, but leave room for a greater love. Strive not by the clasping of arms of flesh to cumber him in the course that he must walk, and the business that the Father has found for him to do.

And as the children round our hearth are a sacred trust, for which we are accountable, so are the children of this whole country a sacred trust to the country at large. It is no misnomer to call a society which undertakes to teach our children the knowledge of God the "*National Society*," for it is at once the symbol and the instrument of a great national duty. It may be that you or I have the means and the will to cause our children to be taught of the Lord. But what shall become of the children of the poor scattered over the

ten thousand parishes of this country? Here is scope
for further efforts. What thanks have you if you
will only guide towards God those whom you love
more than your own life, if your Christian love
reaches no wider than your parental instinct? Not
so was the world redeemed, and afterwards converted to Him who had redeemed it; but by a
love that stretched out its arms to all men, even to
gainsayers. Shall we do nothing for those cases
in which parental love fails? How shall the unin-
structed poor teach their children? They love
theirs as Mary loved her son; if the children were
lost, the parents would seek them sorrowing. But
for higher duties of love they must have help, and
the Society I am pleading for now carries that help
about with it into every quarter. It builds schools
where there were none, in which God's name and
Word shall be taught, in which the knowledge that
is essential to a civilised life is carefully imparted.
Its work is felt in twelve thousand schools, with
more than a million scholars, at this moment. It
does not maintain these schools, but it gives help
at the right moment to aid their erection; it sup-
plies all the instruments and machinery of education; it helps local efforts in maintaining a school
when one has been erected. It has aided largely

H

in providing training‑institutions for teachers, without which no substantial improvement in education could have taken place. Now consider amongst whom this work is done. In a great number of cases amongst the poorest and most neglected of our population. This *Society* does much to wipe away our great national reproach —that children whom we call by the name of Christ, have nothing Christian but the name. We know that Christians must struggle with temptation; but then they must be armed for the struggle and aided in it. .We all remember our Lord's prayer for those He left behind Him: "I pray not that Thou shouldest take them out of the world, but that Thou shouldest keep them from the evil." It is a prayer for those who must contend indeed against evil, but who go out armed with the armour of God against it, and with a hope and a chance of victory. But here in London, as in many other places, one must speak also of those souls, redeemed of Jesus as we have been, that have never risen up so high as to be able even to contend against evil. They are in the world, trampled under its feet, smirched and stained with the pollution of it—*lost* in the sin and evil of it. Oh, mystery of evil! *Souls* that when

He transacted with His Father the redemption of man, were paid for with His blood-drops, more precious than rubies, seem to have been plucked out of His hand, and given into *Satan's* again. Here in this city, with all its riches, its safety for us, its peaceful homes, are nests of people, on whom drink and want and squalid, overcrowded homes, and fever and strife do their worst; whose whole existence is a kind of pushing back from the abhorred brink of starvation. Here you may find, without much seeking, men and women from whose face and form the stamp of God has been almost beaten out. Here are children born and reared in dwellings where decency and sound health are impossible alike, that have never learned anything from parents who have nothing indeed to teach them, who are accustomed to the oath and the brawl, who have often seen, perhaps, a mother's face, battered with blows, and are cunning in keeping out of the reach of a father's drunken right hand. Great mystery of evil! It is beyond our comprehension. Is the hand of God shortened? Was the price of His humiliation too little? Was the gate of heaven shut against that prayer that I have been quoting? Were there some souls too deeply lost for it to reach? How shall we understand these things? We live in a highly civilised country; we look complacently on all the comforts it gives us, and we often indulge in commonplaces about progress, about advancement of our race, and our thoughts have a tincture of pride in them. Ah! look over the sides of that triumphal chariot on which you have written Progress, and see the thousands whom its wheels are crushing to pieces as it rolls, and then be proud. The hands that mixed the mortar for your palaces, and dug underground the ways for the escape of all physical pollution, that you might lodge well and safely— what has progress done for them? It has lighted the gin shop and the street more brightly, and left their dwellings dark. It has made the contrast more intolerable between our easy state and their abject misery. No love, no home, no teaching, no GOD—for His name serves them to swear by, whilst His power they do not know. Might we not almost think that there are some parts of creation that are thoroughly outlawed from God, that the laws of His goodness and His mercy are in abeyance for them? I confess that this subject is the only one connected with the nature of God that baffles while it excites my understanding. I do not wonder that God is omnipotent, that He

hates sin, that the soul shall live for ever, reunited
to a glorified body. But I wonder, and with trembling, that after the Redeemer paid the price, and
a price so past computing, so much of the fruit of
redemption remains still to be gathered. I find it
hard, believing in Calvary, to believe in White-
chapel and St Giles. I find the distance too
infinitely great between Christ at the Father's
right hand, receiving gifts for men, and those dear
to Christ, and by Him redeemed, weltering in sin
and misery, and wretchedness and godless ignorance, in the courts and lanes of the cities of
a Christian land! · Yes, we may wonder, but
not despair. At the door of that dingy room,
where sick and sound are huddled together, there
is a gentle knock, and one enters, as a messenger
from Christ, with the Word of God and of Christ
in his hand, and reads the strange message of salvation; and his tones and looks are full of a
strange compassion; and he will guide the poor
little children, if he is suffered to do so, to a school
where they may be taught to know God. And
the school is open to them freely, that they may
be raised up out of the depths of wretchedness in
which they are sunk, all too deeply. Now, I
know that the Lord has not forgotten them. Even

into that dark dwelling light from above has been
poured. For those lost ones, God is love ; and the
command to us to love one another has a practical bearing, since it brings to that door the
beautiful feet of a messenger of the gospel of
peace.

Brethren, this is the work in which I am to ask
you to help. If you admit that education is a
blessing, this institution claims from you the respect due to every agency in promoting a sound
religious education. Let us be thankful that our
Lord has taught us, both by His example and
precept, reverence for children. He has shown us
a child, still in the age of thoughtless play, seeking the company of the wise, and drawing out
their lessons by intelligent questions. He has
consecrated children by His words, "Suffer the
little children to come unto me." And henceforth our dealings with them must be based upon
this foundation. They are given us that we may
make them love their Father in heaven. Miserable
will be the result of our fondness and our labour
for them, and our indulgence, if we have to deplore
at last that thorns and briers have grown up in
those souls, because we would cultivate nothing
better ; that our bad example, countervailing our

frigid precepts, has made them proud, worldly, indolent, ungodly ; that the seeds of natural corruption in them have been suffered to grow rank, and choke the seed of the Word of Life. We shall then have to complain of ungrateful children that are the blot and the misery of our decline ; but when those erring ones meet us in the day of account, where only truth is spoken, they may complain of us for our neglect of our stewardship, in trifling as we did with souls intrusted to us. Oh ! let us offer them the example of a life pure from evil passions ; let us move out of the way of those uncertain feet, with care the most observant, every stone of stumbling ; let us remind them ever of their glorious birthright, of their place in the kingdom of their Father ; let us be to them, not merely the nourisher of their bodies, but the shepherd of their souls. And if, lifting up our hearts in thanksgiving for a home where peace and love bind us and our children together, we wish to offer to God some tokens of our love for Him, this *Society* is ready to show us the way to make God known in other homes as in our own ; and we shall be doing the will and the work of Christ, the lover of children, the example to children that are to seek their God.

VII.

BY FAITH.

PREACHED AT THE CHAPEL ROYAL, WHITEHALL, ON THE FIRST SUNDAY IN LENT, 1867, AT THE OPENING OF THE SPECIAL LENTEN SERVICES.

"For ye are all the children of God by faith in Christ Jesus."

HOW can faith be the condition of salvation? Why is a man held responsible for his belief or opinion about facts? How can one reconcile those two distinct systems, which bear the common name of Christianity, but have nothing else in common?—the one, that men are judged by God for doing their duty as well as they can; the other, that men are judged according as they accept or reject the account of the salvation of men through Christ. Is not a morality without religion better than a religion without morality? These and similar questions are often asked in our day, which has well been called, for good or for evil, an age of criticism. They are questions that well deserve an answer if we can find one, and the more because they may arise in some cases out of defective and one-sided religious teaching on our part. Let us, this afternoon, try to make some little progress toward an answer; and, for that purpose, let us first have before us a clear statement of the question. May God, the Giver of all knowledge, send the light of His Spirit to guide us!

The question then is this. We are told that we are justified and saved by faith, and not by works. But faith is opinion or belief, and it must belong to the understanding, and not to the heart or the will. If so, then we are justified, counted righteous, not for the moral part of us, the choice we make of good things in preference to evil, not for the state of our affections towards God and holiness, but just for that which least admits of discipline and control—our opinion of the evidence of certain facts; and thus there is a confusion between the moral and the intellectual parts of us, and faith is imputed for righteousness, whereas righteousness and its opposite belong to duty and moral conduct only, and belief should be spoken of not as right or wrong at all, but only as true or mistaken. And whilst natural conscience tells us to judge men by what they do, whilst human laws do the same, religion runs athwart this universal opinion by describing the divine justice as weighing us in another balance and by other weights

than those which conscience uses; and conscience
is surely divine. To make faith the condition of
reconciliation and of eternal life, is to judge by one
small portion of our complex nature, and to leave
the best and most important part out of the great
account between the soul and God.

Such is the difficulty which many feel in trying
to reconcile the language of religious teaching with
the results of their own reasoning and experience.

But I will venture to say that the Bible knows
nothing of this narrow sense of faith. This faith
of the understanding was not the faith described
by Paul. It is true that in comparing law and
gospel, the apostle uses words which seem at first,
when taken alone, to point to a religion that can
dispense with morality. "To him that worketh
not, but believeth on Him that justifieth the ungodly, his faith is counted for righteousness."
These are strong words, meant to be strong, to
strike hard at a strong Jewish prejudice. But in·
the same epistle the rights of morality are abundantly preserved. "The law of the Spirit of life in
Christ Jesus hath made me free from the law of
sin and death." What is this law of the Spirit of
life? It is the indwelling in every saved man of
the Spirit Himself, to inform and quicken the con-

science, and to teach the way of life. "As many as are led by the Spirit of God, they are the sons of God." So then it is not that God takes the ungodly and regards him as godly and just, because of some opinion he has about gospel evidences; but rather that when a man turns to God by faith, God turns to him in love, and gives him the leading and guiding Spirit, and the sense of God's fatherhood, and the peace of forgiveness, and the blessed security of a Father's protection.

Moreover, St Paul shows that it is the love of Christ which gives this power to faith of uniting man with God. "The love of Christ constraineth us," (2 Cor. v. 14.) He died for all, and in this great self-sacrifice we find matter for more than mere belief. Our faith is at once transformed to love and gratitude; in the light of that amazing love, our natures, dull and dark, must yet reflect some of the rays of love that they receive; and so faith is described as "faith that worketh by love." Love is faith in action, and so fulfils the law of Christ. Nor are passages wanting in the epistles of St Paul which recognise that God "will render to every man according to his deeds," (Rom. ii. 6;) "According to that he hath done, whether it be good or bad," (2 Cor. v. 10;) that "whatsoever a man

soweth that shall he reap," (Gal. vi. 7.) Passages
like these seem to be in contradiction at first sight
with those places where the apostle says that none
can be justified by the deeds of the law. But these
passages occur in drawing a contrast between the
Mosaic system and the gospel : the works done
under the law cannot justify ; but, on the other
hand, neither can the faith of the gospel justify,
unless it is transformed into love and hope, and
does the works of the law of Christ, issuing in a
far higher observance than any which the Mosaic
law has reached.

There is, therefore, no countenance in St Paul's
epistles, and if not there, then is there no countenance in the New Testament at all, for the idea
that Christian faith, which justifies, is a single principle, having no connexion but with the understanding. On the contrary, it is a very complex
principle, which leaves no portion of man's com-
posite life unexplored, unchanged. On the contrary, the root of faith spreads into three stems,
faith and hope and charity, and "the greatest of
these" (St Paul says it himself) "is charity." Faith
is religion in our hearts ; and religion means shame
for sin, belief in God's love and power, gratitude
for deliverance, the wish to amend, the endeavour

to bear another's burdens for him, the hope of a nearer approach to God's high presence hereafter. It may indeed be asked how it comes that ideas so vast and various are included under the one name of faith. We shall find the answer most easily in describing faith for ourselves.

We all remember that poor man whom Jesus saw at Capernaum, sitting to receive taxes and custom duties. Nothing can be shorter than the story as it stands: "He saith unto him, Follow me. And he arose, and followed Him." But I think it needs little sagacity to see that that which made this publican do what others of his degraded class thought not of doing, was not a clearer perception of evidences or probabilities, but a moral difference. He wished to become other than he was; some dissatisfaction with his present state had broken down the hedges which usage and prudence would mostly interpose against such a desertion of the calling by which one lives. Was it that he would no more minister to the oppressor above him who farmed the taxes, and grew rich out of the people? Was it that he could not endure the scowls of those in whose wrongs he was the agent? Was it that he had become sensible, from what he had heard of Christ's teaching, of the need of something better for his own soul than what his miserable vocation could furnish? At all events, it was a moral cause, for it altered at once all his life and prospects. It was not that he changed his opinion about Christ, and continued in other respects what he was before. It was an act of the will, and a strong one, which made him leave his office and his means of support, and cast himself upon a vague future, with no guide but Christ. This example serves to explain the share of the will in an act of religious faith. Faith is, as it has been objected, an intellectual act; but also it is a moral act in the next degree. How much or how little of our nature shall be implicated in our belief depends, not on the nature of belief, but upon the objects of it. Last week we believed in an eclipse : it troubled no man's rest, it quickened no man's hopes, it roused no fears, as it might once have done. There was nothing in that object of belief to go down to the heart. Last week we thought that showers of cutting sleet would fall, and in deference to our belief we wrapped another garment round us, or planned a shorter walk. But to believe that a Father's care is over us, and that a higher life is waiting for us, and that a Son has taught us, and for our guilt has died,

and that a life far more noble and beautiful than
we thought, is possible for us even here! Admit such
thoughts in all their force of truth into the outer
hall of our understanding, and their message shall
ring through every passage and chamber, awaken-
ing them that sleep, and quickening with new
strength the hands that hang down in despair.
Belief is mere opinion! Yes; but a belief about
God—about a Father not yet utterly estranged
by all the meanness, selfishness, greedy self-
seeking of one that He will still call His child
—how shall *such* belief be limited to the mere
understanding? No; the whole city within us is
moved at His coming. Affections, feelings, bitter
shames and regrets, fond longings after something better, all stir and troop forth at the mention of such a coming; and they strew their gar-
ments in the way, and throw down the torn
branches in the way, and cry, Hosannah! save us!
to Him that comes to them unexpectedly, blessed
in the name of the Lord. Yes, belief is an opinion;
but that God is and loves us is a great opinion,
and it never dawns upon any understanding but
for great issues.

And though we are not responsible to one another for our belief, surely to God we are respon-

sible. Turn again to the publican whom Jesus called. He had heard much of the new Prophet, of His wonders, such as man had never had power to do; of His sermons, such as man never had grace to utter; of His unheard-of gentleness and meek-ness ; but then he had had much to harden him. To be an agent of fraud and oppression hardens; to be hated for it hardens ; to be forced to bear his master's share of hatred with his own hardens also. There must have come a time when the soul of the man, stiffening by degrees under these deadly influences, must have died there, at his seat and desk, and have become incapable of any nobler act of choice than the exacting of the last farthing that he could collect. But he woke and threw off this numbness before it was too late. Surely, if man is ever responsible, this act of choice was a responsible act. Surely, if he had answered, " I cannot come," guilt would have lain at his door— not, indeed, because the mind is morally respon-sible for dry calculations and inferences from tes-timony, but because, with Jesus calling him, there was reason enough for him to follow, unless some stronger reasons of the heart should keep him back. Cases there may be—there are—where a subtle spirit of inquiry, engendered one knows

not how, forbids a man to rest satisfied in any belief, and detects the weak spot in a chain of proof
however strong.   We must not judge our brother's
belief.   But, in judging ourselves, let us admit that
for our belief we are responsible.   Yes, brethren, if
this Lenten season, in answer to the self-searching
which it suggests, finds us selfish, sensual, lazy,
without God, it is more natural to blame the long
series of selfish acts and thoughts of which to-day's
selfishness is the last link, for our impatience of
belief.   To push the money-taker's table from us,
to feel our heart beat to some other excitement
than those of pleasure, to hasten with free footsteps after the *S*aviour who has called us, require
a nature and a will not wholly corrupt, not utterly
benumbed into sheer necessity of inaction.   This
state of moral feeling was never wrought in
us by doubts about St John's Gospel, by some
notable discovery of Ebionitish influence in
the first age, of which the Acts say nothing.
Admit the truth.   We are too deep sunk in
sin.   Ask not for one to rise from the dead,
that we may believe.   Better far to say the
truth to ourselves, if perchance the awfulness of
the truth may rouse us after all.   Moses, the prophets, Christ himself, have called to us in vain.

Neither should we believe though one rose from the dead.

And now we see why an act in which the whole soul is engrossed bears the name of faith, though faith is one part only of the great change that takes place. Belief or faith is *our* part in the change : the rest follows upon it, and is done for us. If Matthew the publican will rise and follow Christ, his whole life is altered from that moment. He will see Christ daily ; he will be tutored for his part in the work of lifting a world out of sin ; as they journey, he will hear words of wisdom that shall transfigure the trite road, and the old fishing-boat, and the stony shore with something of the light of heaven. He will not be twitted with the past. His new Master receives him as justified by his act of faith, though he requires much training before he can be just. He shall find himself treated as a friend, a brother, by one purer than the angels, wiser than all scribes and doctors. *Daily* he is lifted up more and more out of his old self. Breathing such an air, and refreshed in such a light, he becomes a new creature ; but his share of all that change was the first choice of such a Master, and that choice was made out of trust or faith.

It is now clear that to speak of a religion without morality is as false as to speak of a morality without religion.   No Christian teacher means to separate the two : I wish I could say that none appears to do so.   Faith without works is dead, being alone.   Our faith is one which worketh by love.   A faith that does not produce love and hope is no true faith ; and where these are there is morality, there is glad obedience to the law of Christ.   There may, no doubt, be a morality of a kind that does not belong to any very high or instructed faith.   There may be prudence, fairness, courtesy, temperance, family affection, amongst those who do not pretend to study Christian faith, and even speak lightly of such a study.   Are they without faith, however ?   There are in their lives, perhaps, many signs of a belief in a higher law than mere social calculations, and to that extent they live by faith.   Those who do not mean to walk in the full light of the Sun of Righteousness are guided by His reflected light.   The code of honour, the rules of courtesy, are founded on the law of Christ.   Respect for women, respect for truth, an unselfish surrender of our own desires and advantages in little things—where would these have been but for the old tables of stone, but for

the sermon on the mount? But the morality of a
real faith ought to be far brighter than these faint
reflections of it. Shame upon believers if it be not
so! Believers have before them a heavenly Father
who cannot endure sin, who desires their sanctifi-
cation. They have a measure of the depth of sin
such as we find nowhere else; sin was that which
looked upon the very face of Christ, the blessed Son,
and hated Him when it saw Him, cursed Him,
smote Him, put Him to death, with the crying witness of His miracles and His holiness to tell them
they were striking at God. Sin was that deep-seated
evil which none could cure but He who was alone
sinless, and even He by nothing short of death.
Seeing the foulness of the taint, and its persist-
ence, they should surely watch and pray even
against the faintest spot of that plague, against
the lightest whisper of its temptations. Believers,
again, have a cogent motive for crucifying self and
selfish wishes, in the remembrance of what Christ
did for them. The Master whom they serve may
well call on them to bear each other's burdens, and
to do to others what they would wish to receive
from them, for He did indeed bear their burdens.
"Let this mind be in you which was in Christ
Jesus." If it could be shown that the gospel of

faith in Jesus Christ was no longer producing
fruits of special holiness, then would the tree be
dead, and would cumber the ground, and might
be cut down. But every hospital, refuge, reformatory, ragged school, mission—every attempt of
one class to ennoble another—bears witness to the
life of that tree of faith. And call it a paradox if
you will, still it is a fact, that nowhere is there
more activity in well-doing than there where all
merit of activity is renounced, and the mind turns
to God as to the sole source of all forgiveness,
life, peace, holiness.

Nor have those attempts which are constantly
made to fasten upon St Paul and St James a
contradiction, as though the one exalted faith
and banished works, and the other exalted works
by degrading faith, been at all successful. The
one condemned works that had no faith in them ;
the glittering counterfeits of obedience with which
the Pharisees sought to buy God's favour, by
measure and by weight. The other denounced
the faith which did not touch the life and bear
fruit. It has been well said * that the two writers
opposed, not each other, but each a different kind
of hypocrisy—the one that of the law, and the

* By Vinet. Etudes Evangéliques.

other that of faith. Is either of these extinct?
Men sometimes say, " We want neither prayers,
nor lectures, nor Bible, nor Church, to tell us what
to do ; we do our duty, and that is enough." And
others say, " We are godly people, justified, saved,
and works matter little, and are rather a snare ; so
we will do nothing, but leave all to God." I know
not which errs the most. Christian holiness is a
goodly tree ; they have cut it in two, and one has
kept the root, and the other some of the branches,
but the tree is not.

If I had meant to speak of the theory of faith
and works, I must have admitted that, after all
these explanations, a mystery remains. How to
reconcile God's goodness with man's activity, providence with freedom, love with the existence of
evil,—these are questions which have exercised
the best minds from the beginning. But they are
not Christian questions. Rabbis knew them—
philosophers felt their force. If we cannot con-
ciliate the thesis and the antithesis which seem
always to spring up together, let us try to reconcile
them in practice. In practice the difficulty dis-
appears. When Paul says, " Work out your own
salvation with fear and trembling, for it is God
which worketh in you both to will and to do of

His good pleasure," (Phil. ii. 12, 13,) no understanding can reconcile these opposite views of human working; but in practice the seeming contradiction gives no trouble. The work is ours, yet God's. It is the practical aspect of this question that belongs most to this season of Lent. However else we may observe it, let us give some part of our time to the endeavour to renew our faith before God, to lifting our hearts nearer to Him, to the offering Him all that we are or can do. Each time has had its trials, and this time is especially adverse to that complete overruling faith which shapes a life wholly for God. We may be religious a little —nay, religion is the subject most discussed. But to rise and follow Christ because He is the Son of God, because He has saved the world, is hard, for a thousand whispers round us forbid us to go that length. Men smite Christ under cover of saluting Him; and I think that more fatal to all high faith are the grudging praises, and the patronising tones wherewith men now let themselves speak of Christ the Lord, than words of mere hostility, though they be sharp as swords. Yet we are the children of God by faith in Christ Jesus. We are not so much churchmen, or believers in Christianity, as we are followers of Christ. Oh, that God may

give us that great peace—of lifting us for a while
out of ourselves—out of the strange distractions of
our social state—to calm us, and comfort us, and
to send us back with a fresh assurance of what He
would have us do! As it were from the Mount of
Transfiguration, we shall come down again from
that shining presence with these three ideas
printed strongly in our hearts—obedience to God,
love to men, the hope of life eternal—to interpret
to us our task in the world. We are in peril from
luxury and from unbelief. Riches are great
amongst us, and they have their usual effect. A
belief that strong wine cheers, and that good
meats are sweet, and that exciting books and
sports beguile the heaviness of time, is easy
enough; but a race that so believes is sinking
into corruption, and would soon disappear. Out
of a world that threatens to stifle us with its
luxurious indulgence, its light contempt for high
subjects and motives, let us cry to the Lord that
has saved us—Lord, I believe; help thou my
unbelief! And faith can save us still—faith that
ever renews itself by returning to its Lord, and
laying down self and selfish wishes before Him,
asks to know His will, and to have strength given
to keep it.

VIII.

THE SPIRIT OF WORSHIP.

PREACHED IN LICHFIELD CATHEDRAL, IN 1865, AT
MEETING OF CHOIRS.

" And Jacob awaked out of his sleep, and he said, Surely the Lord
is in this place; and I knew it not. And he was afraid, and
said, How dreadful is this place! this is none other but the
house of God, and this is the gate of heaven."

THINKING only perhaps of the refreshment
of sleep, Jacob laid down his wearied head
upon a pillow of stone in Bethel. In a vision
which, by the very awe that it brought to him, was
distinguished from a common dream, God spake
to the sleeping traveller, and told him great things
that should be. The words of my text were what
he uttered when morning broke. God had been
there with him speaking to his soul; and now awe
and reverence belonged to that place. In his zeal
he made a pillar out of the stones on which he
had rested; and after that symbolic building he
called the place Bethel, the house of God.

God dwells not in temples made with hands;
God is everywhere. He who is bent on finding
God needs not seek Him in the stately cathedral,

needs not the apparatus of ornament and music, when he would draw near Him. The devoted missionary drooping daily on the mephitic shores of the African river, knows God's comforting presence in his death, although there is no church for him to worship in, and scarcely one other believer near to say Amen when he shall pray. Were our hearts all fixed upon God, we should need no church, as in the New Jerusalem there shall be no temple; and instead of appointing a minister to conduct our prayer, and training choirs to praise Him, we should hear from all His creatures one great harmony of praise to the Lord of all. God would have shone out for man from the heaven of stars rounded over His head, from the enamelled meadow jewelled with wild flowers, from the vast and restless sea, from the strong oak and the thin lichen, from the lion in the forest, and the silkworm in its silken prison, from the man's conscious intellect, and the instinct of the ant and the bee. Men full of thoughts of God would have found Him everywhere. But they had turned from Him; and amidst a world that sung of God, that spoke aloud of His glory and goodness, the brutish eyes of man ceased to look for Him. Instead of going forth towards Him with loving admiration,

and giving Him thanks for all that He had done,
man, in his self-worship, thought only of the world
in connexion with his convenience. He looked
on the universe, not as a temple of the living God,
but as a kitchen and a workshop for the comfort of
man. Vain then was the summons, " The Lord
is in his holy temple : let all the earth keep silence
before him," (Hab. ii. 20.) The Lord was still in
His temple ; but selfishness cannot co-exist with
reverence. And man, all unconscious of God,
strutted and wrangled and strove for his little hour
upon the floor of the temple, before the very holy
of holies. Then helps were needed to remind this
thoughtless creature of One whose power over·
him was absolute, whose love towards him was
as great as His power. One day of seven was
marked for the Lord, to whom all days should belong. A house, a temple, a church, is set apart
for Him, whose throne is heaven above, whose
footstool is the earth beneath, that, at least
there where His name is called, poor weak men
may collect their scattered minds, and fix them
upon something beyond and above themselves.
Brethren, this is the rationale of all worship of our
God and Lord. What can we add to God, even by
building for Him the most stately cathedral that

K

the brain of the architect ever projected? What
can we profit Him by adding our trained voices to
the spontaneous hymns of angels far away, in singing His praise? Nothing to Him. The temple
and the praises are much to us, but to Him that
sitteth upon the throne all glory belongs already,
and He needs not our witness. All creation is His;
and the very heavens with their brightness are too
sordid for Him. Why then should He need such
houses as we can build, or look with favour on the
artist's skill, when He made the artist and all his
types in nature, and moulded secretly in the earth
even the block from which the corner-stone was
hewn? Worship is for man's edification; it can
add nothing to God.

Brethren, no one can have attended many of
our churches in past years without seeing too
plainly that man's indolence and selfishness may
creep even into his worship. The Church, totter-
ing, uncared for, smelling of mildew, blotched with
damp, opened its doors to a few worshippers, to
whom the very notion of common prayers—of
prayer offered by a loving brotherhood, emulous
to show their love to the Lord who had redeemed
them all alike—seemed entirely strange. Secluded
by twos and threes in separate cells, which they

were prepared sternly to defend against all invasion, they heard the minister and clerk confess,
and added no word of their own to that vicarious
penitence ; they allowed the psalms—those rich
treasures of devout feeling and experience, provided by the Holy Spirit for the wants of the
Church in all ages—to be said in alternate verses
by the same deputies ; they listened to hymns
sung by tuneless children in some distant corner.
And this was worship. These were the voices of
zeal with which the bride of Christ addressed the
beloved Bridegroom, earnestly desiring His return.
That Church, with its ignoble makeshifts and dank
discomfort, was meant to symbolise God's throne
and presence to those who could not find Him in
the glories—ever bright and fresh, because ever
renewed by the Creator himself—of the world
without ! Those tame and frigid utterances were
supposed to be the outgoings of united hearts in
love and praise towards Him whom they loved
because of the hope of redemption. If that sad
day has passed away, there is much to be thankful
for. If churches are now seemly or beautiful; if
the voice of the congregation is heard in penitent
submission, in praise, in thanksgiving ; if the music
of the sanctuary is such as encourages devout feel-

ings; if the high ramparts of the church-pew, raised to show that even in church, before God, men had not equal rights, were not equal, are crumbling down, not from any violent onslaught, but from the tacit conquest of better ideas, there is much to be thankful for.

And such a day as this, in which many hundreds of worshippers, at much trouble and cost, are gathered together, from various parts of this large diocese, with the express object of making our parochial worship more solemn and edifying, has much comfort in it. Yet let us not in this presence glorify ourselves. Let us rather think upon the dangers and temptations to which we, poor sinners that we are, are exposed even in the worship of God, our holiest employment. Let us remember how poor and savourless is all worship in which awe and humility and love are wanting. Wasted indeed, and worse than wasted, would our labour be for improving our church worship, if instead of dull carelessness we substituted only a mechanical exactness. The Christian creed knows no sacrifice, since the perfect oblation of Christ, except the offering of our hearts in love and gratitude to Him who has redeemed us.

1. When we worship in God's house, He is pre-

sent. Surely the Lord is in this place; and I
knew it not. This is none other but the house of
God, and this is the gate of heaven. . . . . The
Lord is in His holy temple; let all the earth keep
silence before Him. We have chosen and set
apart this place for our most sacred intercourse
with God. Here the heart lays bare its sins in
words of deepest sorrow. Here we listen with
eager ears for the news of forgiveness. Here we
commend to God the Church, the throne, the
world's peace, the prospects of those we love, the
various classes of tried and suffering people. For
all these we call upon God; and if He be not present to hear, our whole worship is without a meaning.
The Lord is in this place! Oh! words full of rebuke to many a thoughtless worshipper that enters
without much thought of God. Oh! words that
rebuke even those who are passive, and have no
earnest purpose in the presence of Him whom
they need. Oh! words of shame to those who,
when they are here, open the doors of their mind
to all kinds of thoughts, pure and impure; who
complete last week's calculations, or settle next
week's business, or dwell upon their covetousness
or their impurity with a morose delight. Who is
God, whom we thus set at nought, invoking His

presence and then despising it? The Psalmist represents all nature as bowing down in awe before His might. By His strength He sets fast the mountains, He stills the noise of the waves and the madness of the people. He divides the sea by His strength. At His rebuke both the chariot and horse are cast into a dead sleep. The waters see Him and are afraid. All earthly creatures wait upon Him, and He giveth them their meat in due season. He hides His face, they are troubled; He takes away their breath, they die, and return to their dust. He sends forth His Spirit, they are created, and He reneweth the face of the earth. This is the God whom we so despise, whose presence we seek so thoughtlessly; the God whom heaven, and earth, and every creature, man excepted, wait upon and obey; the God in whom we live, and move, and have our being; the God whose strength is lent to us or we should perish—who makes our pulse beat, strengthens our sinews, gives light and thought to our brain; the God who is so close to us that we are shut up in His very hand, we mock Him with sham worship, and there, upon the threshold of that awful presence, the full glory of which is veiled from us or we should perish, we have no thought of awe or rever-

ence ; and whilst the words of inspiration are
spoken to His praise, we yawn, or wander, or ogle,
or scheme to pass away the time, forsooth, which
else would be entirely vacant. Yes; let the knee
bow visibly at the name of Jesus, but the heart
bowing and reverent before the great God and
Lord, and before His Christ, is what the believer
should bring here when he would worship. To
feel, when we are here, the great overshadowing
presence of the Rock of Ages, a cooling shadow
in a weary land, a safe shelter from the storm ; to
be saved by that thought from all wanderings of
spirit, all mean calculations, all foul desires ; to be
possessed by the thought of God, so that other
thoughts can find no room in us ; this is Christian
worship. How dreadful is this place! This is
none other than the hand of God, and this is the
gate of heaven.

2. But I have spoken only of that awe which
the creature feels towards its Creator and Pre-
server, which the Psalmist in those sublime strains
attributes also to floods and skies, to beast and
feathered fowl. But the earth that trembled and
shook before Thee, the waves that were afraid of
Thy thunder, had never *sinned* against Thee. Man
comes into Thy presence, not so much a creature

acknowledging its constant dependence upon its creator, as a sinner confessing that he has lost his inheritance of purity and fallen away from Thee. What we come here to seek is not merely present help, but safety at the last. We come not to assert a right or a power, but to implore forgiveness. We come not to give an account of our doings, as faithful stewards of God, which will bear the most searching scrutiny, but as prodigal sons who have gone far astray, and are no more worthy to be called His sons. What, then, should the tone of our devotion be? Shall we be careless? Life is passing; the grave is open; there is a judgment; eternity is long. If we fear Him because He speaks in storm and thunder, because His breath gives life to the world, because all the suns and worlds scattered through the space of creation, which no human thought can count or measure, are all the work of His word, we must fear Him rather because there is that upon our souls which He cannot love or take to Himself. When we join the company of holy angels, and of just men made perfect, to praise God and pray to Him, we ought to feel as some leper, with sordid rags half covering his loathsome sores, that comes into a king's banquet to sit down side by side with princes. Shall we find nothing to move us in a service that speaks throughout of this sin, and of redemption from it? Shall we find room in our minds for the pride of dress, or for care about good seats, from which the poor are excluded, or for ancient feuds with the minister, or the like, when our Lord regards us as poor lost creatures, desiring in our misery to be fed with the crumbs from His table. Yes, we must needs be humble in the house of God, when all the service speaks of penitence, pardon, reconciliation; when, above all, the infinite humility of Christ was made the means of our redemption. He sat on His throne of glory in heaven, and far down below Him lay the race of men, in the prison of sin, sick with every form of lust and violence and disorder. He can sweep away by a word all this plague spot that flecks the brightness of His shining universe. There need be no man to spoil it with his wilful selfishness; nothing but bright stars that run their course in glad obedience to Him; and flowers that blow and wither at His will; and seas whose storms and calms are but the acting of His thought, His law. Man, that nothing will tame or mend; man, that has been tried for centuries and has ever got worse; man, of whom creation is weary, because

of his violence and corruption ; let him be destroyed, and another race be created upon the
scene that he has disfigured and dishonoured.
Not so: He will descend from that high throne,
He will lay aside the robe of His glory, He will
become one of that race of whom the very earth
and heaven were weary. In the form of a servant
He will accept whatever of insult, wrong, suffering,
they choose to lay upon Him. He will die—even
die—to purchase back the forfeited favour of His
Father for this lost race, that shall slay Him in
hatred for His reward. That is the story which
comes before us in every service of our Church.
At least it should make us humble worshippers of
Him who thus has commended humility to us.

3. And lastly, Our worship should abound in
love. The boundless love of Jesus wins us to that.
He has forgiven us all. It is no longer as despair-
ing outcasts that we think of God. No ; we add
our praises to those of the angels, as the redeemed
of the Lord, to be numbered hereafter with the
angelic company, with prophets, saints, and mar-
tyrs. The great down-streaming light of love
from on high disperses the darkness of our hearts,
and we feel that we are not lost. When our
gloomy spirit cries, "I have sinned against the

Lord," a voice from on high makes answer, " The
Lord hath put away thy sin." Is it not a miserable narrowness and littleness that men can come
into a church nursing some petty parish feud,
jealous of some neighbour in the next pew, turning his eyes by force away lest he should have to
speak to one whom he has kept up a studied ani-
mosity against for many a long year? Know you
whose you are? You belong to One whose name
is Love. If He had been angry where it was due,
eternal death had been our portion. Kneel, then,
before Him, and think of the love that made Him
lay down His life for His friends. Friends He
calls you; but this again is out of His love. He
laid down His life for foes and sinners. After that
thought, if you are sincere in it, all petty feuds and
differences fade away out of your minds. We are
kneeling at the feet of our greatest benefactor
Lord! what wilt Thou have us do in return for
love such as none have ever shown us? It is Himself that answers, "As I have loved you, that ye
also love one another," (John xiii. 34.)

Let me speak, in conclusion, a word to those
who have come here to lend solemnity by their
voices and their skill to this day's act of worship.
You have indeed been doing a good work. You

wish to turn the tame and listless singing of God's
praises, which used to be the rule, into a hearty
outpouring of devoted love; so that when we meet
for worship your zeal may stir up others' zeal, as
iron sharpeneth iron. Already the good effect is
felt in many a village church, in the larger congregations of our towns. Men are not ashamed to
praise God. They no longer think it proper to
have their praise of their great God and Lord sung
for them, and ill sung. Go on then in this your
work, for it is good indeed. The tame, frigid,
drawling, tuneless, tasteless psalmody of times
now passing away made worship a penance rather
than a pleasure; and you are resolved to replace
it by something which devout hearts may find a
support and not a hindrance. Oh, my friends, if you
would make this your ministry complete, sanctify the Lord God in your hearts. It is because I
see the great value of this movement that I warn
you against its dangers. Let us not change a carelessness about all outward worship for a frigid perfection of ritual to which the heart is wanting.
Let us not make the choir a stage on which our
vanity may display itself. I have heard that
sometimes the praises of God have been unsung
upon His holy day because the singers had chosen

that mode of avenging some fancied slight on the part of the minister; and so, because man had offended them, they declined to praise God. But you are servants, not of man, but of God, great and awful, throned in heaven; you are sinners who must seek His pardon; you are followers of Jesus, because you admire the wonders of His love. How shall you find room for petty malignity, for self-love, for careless wandering fancies, when you are God's servants, singing praise to Him for redemption from the terrors of hell?

I beseech you, be not content until you are godly men, meet for this excellent ministry you have undertaken. There will come a day, whether near or distant no man can tell you, when the world, weary with its long course, shall slacken and stand still, and all this solid Church, glorious and beautiful, shall crumble away, and the very heavens over us shall shrivel and disappear. Then all human wisdom and skill shall cease, and the most beautiful singing shall be silenced. Yet not the worship of those who, out of loving hearts, have sung the praise of God with understanding. The angels would miss that kind of worship if it were silenced. It has been rising from the earth, a small voice and yet a clear, and has mixed in

harmony with the very song of the angels, and
with the music of their harps. The prayers of
saints on earth have reached the throne already;
they are the odours in the golden vials of the prophetic vision. Your voices then have reached
heaven and the throne of the Lamb already; they
shall not perish nor be lost. The very angels
would bid you come up and join them. No more
to sing praise to God under cloudy skies, amid
much temptation, amid much weakness, in temples
made with hands, beautiful indeed, but mere sha-
dows and feeble copies of beauty; but in the new
heaven, where there is no sin, nor suffering, nor
feebleness, nor failing, to sing salvation to our God
which sitteth upon the throne, and unto the Lamb.
God hath this day lifted our thoughts to that
blessed country: may He bring us there to dwell
with Him for ever!

IX.

THE NIGHT COMETH.

PREACHED AT BUCKINGHAM PALACE, BEFORE THE QUEEN, THE PRINCE CONSORT, AND THE KING OF THE BELGIANS, 1858.

"I must work the works of Him that sent me, while it is day : the night cometh, when no man can work."

THESE are solemn words, and every one may make them his own, without drawback or alteration. Every one was sent into the world with a task appointed for him : the path of every one's life leads him before long into the thick shadow and night of the grave. But how wonderful they are as spoken by the Lord Jesus! He, too, owns that He is sent to carry through a work, and that the appointed time for its performance is passing away. Yes ; it was even so. The Church which He founded, and which, without sound of axe or hammer, has ever since been growing, with its foundations upon the broad ages, and with converted men for its stones, Jesus Himself being the Head of the corner, with the wise spirits of the earth for its pillars, and the prayers of the saints for its incense, this great moral edifice is, so to

L

speak, the fruit of a man's work, even of that of the
Son of Man. We are not told that He spake the
word only, and it was made : it was not by a voice
coming down from a region of sublime repose into
the stirring universe, that the religion of Christ
was established upon earth, to console the penitent, and repress sin, and build up holiness. In
the truest sense, it is the fruit of the labour of Him
who cheerfully accepted this as His appointed task
on earth. In three years—for such at most was
the duration of His ministry—those journeyings,
and sermons, and parables, those fastings and
night-watchings, those persecutions, those miracles
that conquered sickness and the grave, that agony,
that death, that resurrection, were all completed.
Grappling with the reality of sorrow, facing the
baffling opposition which He might have scattered
with the breath of His displeasure, He " wrought
the works of Him that sent Him while it was day."
Truly, He did take on Him the form of a servant,
and was made in the likeness of men. The light
of His doctrine, of His great atoning sacrifice, of
His sinless character, have been shining on the
world ever since ; and men have been willing to
rejoice in that light. But not like the natural
light was the spiritual kindled. We do not read,

"Christ said, Let there be light, and there was light." He speaks of struggle, and labour, and conflict; He speaks such words as these :—"I have a baptism to be baptized with; and how am I straitened till it be accomplished!" (Luke xii. 50.) "Now is my soul troubled; and what shall I say? Father, save me from this hour: but for this cause came I unto this hour," (John xii. 27.)

And it is by work that the kingdom of Christ must spread. I speak not only of such labourers as St Paul or St Peter, as Augustine or Luther, of those mighty spirits who have been able to write their names on a nation converted, or a great truth fixed permanently in the treasury of Christian thought, or a great error exposed, saying, "This God did through me." There is a work for each and all. Men tell us that in the material world there is no particle lost or useless; not a tiny pebble is there whose mass does not contribute its share to that attraction which keeps planet true to sun, and satellite to planet; not a gust blows, nor a wave falls back in foam from the shore, but leaves its mark upon the changing face of nature. What God has made the law of nature He wills to be the law of the moral world also. No soul so meek, no will so dependent, but was meant to take a part in

that progress of mind and spirit which is moving
parallel to the progress of nature. Oh what a
misfortune it must be, then, to a man to have a
low conception of his duty and work in the world !
What a misfortune, if he fancy that he has no
work here to do ! Parts we are, each of us, of the
world that rolls on, neither resting nor hasting, to
the end which the Maker has appointed for it.
The material frame of man has taken up a portion
of the dust of it, and is ever moulding and transforming it ; his cogent animal wants drive him to
dig and reap, hunt and fish ; and so far his work is
done. But the gift of an immortal spirit is often
entrusted to one who never tries to discover what
are the duties that attach to that most excellent
possession. What a misfortune that the highest
part of us should be the barrenest ! that our value
as factors in the grand sum of the universe should
be only our weight as shaped clods of earth, or our
worth as animals seeking for a provision ! No one
but thinks such a result of life would be deplorable.
No one but will pardon a few plain words on a
subject which, if it has been handled by ten
thousand preachers, can never, so long as the
safety of souls is knit up with it, be thought
obsolete.

I. All that has been done for the human race in the way of bringing the news of redemption to them, or of freeing them from the miseries that sin brought into the world, has been, by God's direct permission and ordinance, the result of individual effort. Not without reason did our Redeemer choose the way of labour and diligence as that by which He would approach the Father to make atonement for us. His great example has never been without its fruit from the earliest time. Next to the history of the blessed Redeemer Himself, the largest page in the New Testament is that which records the doings of St Paul.. Ceaseless activity, indomitable boldness, a deep love for human souls, brought him into contact with every form of worship, every stage of human culture, every climate that lay within the reach of a traveller at that time. And when, in no boastful spirit, he puts before the Church at Corinth the bare record of his life, which passes as of itself into a rhythmic cadence, we are constrained to confess that that terrible hymn of suffering and labour is surely the meetest praise that ever a mortal man could offer to his God; for it is the plain story of a laborious and much-suffering life, every portion of which was dedicated to the Giver of all life and all good. "In labours more abundant, in stripes above measure, in prisons more frequent, in deaths oft. Of the Jews five times received I forty stripes save one. Thrice was I beaten with rods, once was I stoned, thrice I suffered shipwreck, a night and a day I have been in the deep. In journeyings often, in perils of waters, in perils of robbers, in perils by my own countrymen, in perils by the heathen, in perils in the city, in perils in the wilderness, in perils in the sea, in perils among false brethren; in weariness and painfulness, in watchings often, in hunger and thirst, in fastings often, in cold and nakedness. Beside those things that are without, that which cometh upon me daily, the care of all the churches," (2 Cor. xi. 23-28.) But even the *silent* labours of the other Apostles—for of their doings, except those of Peter, John, and Paul, the New Testament says but little—have their eloquence for us; they, too, travelled and preached, and poured out their blood for a witness, without recording even in the simplest way what they were doing, and what they were about to suffer. But their works remain. There is a record kept by a pen that writes only truth, on a page that no moth nor worm shall eat, until the day of judgment; and there it is written that whosoever else may have abused his talent, they made usury of theirs, and shall enter for ever into the joy of their Lord.

And if we leave the Apostles, men so specially helped by the Spirit of God that their works may seem scarcely to be examples for us, so far above us do they appear, does not every age abound with the fruits of labour of the *Divine Spirit* working in men an active zeal for God? Individual piety and self-denial raised the village church and the vast cathedral, and bequeathed them to the flock of Christ without money and without price. Individual piety founded the college and the school, expressly dedicated to Christian teaching; and raised the hospital, in order that one prominent mark of the kingdom of Christ, the care for the sick and weak, might there be, as it were, graven in stone. When our prisons had become so many sinks of physical and moral corruption, one man explored the disease and procured the remedy. Two or three persons were able, God helping them, to clear our nation from the guilt of the slave-trade, although the love of gain resisted to the utmost. The movement in favour of education for the poor began but lately and from a few. The rescue of outcast women from a hopless depth of degradation has been attempted by a few, and found possible. The reformatory for the young criminal, now the subject of interest to the whole country, is one of the latest outgrowths of Christian love, and at first but one or two had found the secret out. And who were these, who, in the Spirit of the Lord, have been strong enough for such heroic deeds, and brought back such rich trophies from the battle with Satan? Were they only the very wise, or the very rich, or the very influential? Far from it. In the catalogue of such heroes we shall find the names of men and women of every grade and station, some of them poor enough, of narrow education, quite unknown in the world, abounding in nothing except patience and love. Who is there who cannot imitate them? Vain are the complaints so often made, that we have no distinct work in life appointed for us; that we stand idle because we have not been called into the vineyard to labour. God has made duties for us, and placed us in the midst of them, just as He has made light for the eyes, and air for us to breathe. There is not an action of our life that may not become an act of worship, if it is consecrated by the love of God in the heart of the doer. But the common round of our common daily life is full of occasions of Christian duty. I think that when Jesus, the Redeemer of the human race, preached the glories and the terrors of the world to come, sitting in a fisher's boat on a retired lake in a province of the Jewish country which was a byword amongst the Jews themselves, to an untaught multitude thronging the shore, He showed us not merely that He loved our kind and would save them, but also, that wherever a man's lot is cast, there is the place where God's work should be done. The first words of the Gospel message were confided to a few unlettered persons, who in the beginning understood them imperfectly, and failed to remember them; yet we do not find, because the mustard-seed was sown in obscure Judæan soil, that the tree is weak, or unfit for shelter. Who is he that stands idle because he is not hired? One it must be who can find neither poverty, nor ignorance, nor wickedness at his hand; who cannot influence one person by the Christian tone of his own life; who cannot sweeten the daily life of his home with kindness; who never comes near a sinner rushing headlong to his ruin; who cannot even find a child to encourage in struggling with an evil tem-

per, nor a stricken heart to be consoled by a word
of sympathy. On some desolate island, shared
only with the bird of the air and the beast of the
forest, such an isolated being might possibly be
found; but even for that outcast, if he sought the
Lord, work would be appointed; and in a closer
communion with God, in prayer, and praise, and
trust, his soul would find its exercise, and the
means of its discipline and purification. The life
that is shaped according to the pattern of Christian duty out of a heart full of Christian faith and
love, sends up to God day by day a perpetual
voice of praise; and whether it comes before men
from a high and illustrious position, or hides itself
in some obscure corner where few can follow it,
the equal eye of God discerns in both cases alike,
that here is one working the work of Him that
sent him whilst it is day. God grant in mercy to
all of us a deep sense of the sacredness of our life,
and an earnest resolution to consecrate to Him all
that we are, and do, and think!

II. For "the night cometh when no man can
work." This truth has been dwelt on by Christian and heathen teachers since the world was
young. The pages of the Old Testament are full

of it: but never was it uttered with a more solemn sanction than when He spake it who could not be holden of death. The night cometh: to some it comes as the night of nature, with slow, regular, and foreseen steps; on some it drops suddenly, when they thought it was noon; for some life becomes, what with feeble health and blunted powers, one long twilight. For it is not death only which is our night; where the opportunity has been lost, there the night has settled already. *D*eath may be far from many of us: the journey may be long and weary before our sun goes down. But do we take no account of smaller deaths, so to speak? *D*o we not feel the dreadful suspicion that part of us may be dead already? Are we not conscious of changes that are in their way final? *D*o we not pass every year on our life's journey some landmark which we shall wish to see again, and shall not be able? That memory which now records for us every fact we entrust to it, night comes upon it, when it will be less faithful. That quickness of conscience, which now punishes with remorse each sin of impurity or violence, night will come upon it if we despise it, and the gnawings of each new sin against the callous heart shall be unfelt. That

friend or neighbour with whom we take sweet
counsel, let us learn from him all we can, let us
pour out for him all the truth we know, and let
heart strengthen heart as iron sharpeneth iron ; for
we may see him again no more for ever, and in his
stead nothing but recollections shall remain, over-
shadowed with the night of a grievous loss. Teach
the child whilst he is spared you, for the angel may
gather that flower into one of his sheaves, to plant
him again in the radiance of the *D*ivine throne,
leaving you to the trial of a numbed and benighted
affection. Oh, the unspeakable misery that it will
be to review all the lost chances of a life that is as
changeful as the restless sea ! Hope at present
with most of us overrules memory ; in what we
may yet do, we lose sight of all that we might
have done. When we reach the confine of life'
and no food for earthly hope remains ; when before us is nothing brighter than the valley of the
shadow of death ; then shall the bitterness of all
past deaths and losses deepen tenfold the shadow
that is settling over us. How prodigal we were of
time when we should have been misers of it ! How
we let the friend drift from us with a careless fare-
well, ignorant that then and there, the commerce
that might have been so fruitful for both was

ended for evermore! How often we uttered the
hasty word, when silence would have become us
better! How we kept silence from good words,
when an honest expression of opinion would have
checked folly or sin! How gladly we saw our
precious years buried one by one in the bosom of
an eternity that never gives back its dead! Oh,
let us no longer squander our treasures of opportunity! God has placed us upon this narrow
island of time, with the waters of eternity all
around us; and every inch of ground is more
precious to us than gold or rubies; for, as our
dealings with time are, so our share of immortality
shall be. And we can make no terms with Him
to grant us a longer season to finish the work He
sent us to do. The night cometh, and it shall
overtake the thinker before he has matured his
discovery, and the ruler in the midst of plans of
order and improvement. Let us set before us
every morning the preciousness of a new day
granted to us out of the long night that shall
follow, that we may work in it the work of Him
that sent us. Let us work, henceforth, not our
own works, but the work of Him that sent us. Let
us teach our children to know Him. Let us make
our own lives a witness to the truth, as if some

light from another world had indeed broken forth
for us upon the rough and gloomy places of this,
and had guided our feet aright, whosoever else had
stumbled. Let us be covered with shame, if in
times past we have trifled with our trust. Let us
seek to combat those evils which our social state
tends to produce, and which, without the mitigat-
ing force of Christian love, would reach an intolerable height. Let us try to do men good in the
name of that Father who crowns them with mercy
and loving-kindness; let us try to turn their eyes
to the redemption wrought by the Son; let us
promote love among them in the name of the
Spirit of truth, and comfort, and love. And re-
membering that God alone can turn the night that
is coming upon us into a most glorious day, if we
seek Him here whilst He may be found, let us pray
to Him fervently, "So teach us to number our
days, that we may apply our hearts unto wisdom,"
(Ps. xc. 12.)

X.

PRAYER.

PREACHED AT BUCKINGHAM PALACE BEFORE THE QUEEN
AND THE PRINCE CONSORT, 1860.

"And in that day ye shall ask me nothing. Verily, verily, I say unto you, Whatsoever ye shall ask the Father in my name, he will give it you. Hitherto have ye asked nothing in my name: ask, and ye shall receive, that your joy may be full."

THESE words bring before us the whole mystery of prayer. The gift of God is made to depend upon the prayer of man. "Whatsoever ye shall ask the Father in my name, he will give it you." The treasures of earth and heaven belong to the Lord, but He seems here to put into the hands of man the key of prayer to unlock them at his pleasure. Can it be so? Can I ask for the place of honour in the kingdom, for the wealth that may be an instrument of good, for the intellect that adorns goodness and commands the world to honour it, for the fire from heaven that will destroy my enemies, for the removal far from me of the eager pains and gnawing aches that torment so many sufferers, for a life that shall be one unruffled stream of happiness and enjoyment;

M

and will He give me all these in the name of His blessed Son? And if He will give these, or any of them, does He not in effect make over the government of His world to me? It seems impossible to conceive how God can answer a human prayer consistently with His own foreknowledge and power as governor of the universe. For if prayer could heal the sick, then the withholding of prayer would leave them unhealed; if prayer can draw down the grace of God into the heart of a man, and so change his whole life and ways of action, then his neglecting to pray would have left him in his old condition; and this alternative would affect not merely himself, but all who might live within his influence, a family, a parish, the crew of a ship, the inhabitants of a country. And thus a certain measure of control over the affairs of the world is left to the will of man. Can anything be made dependent upon prayer, yet form part of God's wise and settled government of the world? This question does indeed contain a mystery, and one which we shall never solve here below. We may stand gazing before the veil, but our eyes have no power to pierce it, and until it is rolled away at last, that we may see face to face, we shall not find an answer for our doubt.

But it is no new difficulty which Christianity has
brought in. It is only a part of that larger question which would have been discussed by sages if
the gospel had never been preached, which would
have been as hard to solve even if no prayer had
ever been offered. I mean the question, How can
God's wisdom, settling all beforehand, leave any
room for that freedom of choice which we all feel
in ourselves, and which we assume to exist in all
others? When a king takes up the pen to sign an
instrument that makes a people free; when a
general resolves to hazard a battle, the victory of
which shall bring back peace to a quarter of the
world; when it rests with a Luther whether, at
peril of his life, he will speak strong words that
shall echo down the ages, or weakly hold his
peace: then, in such decisive moments, we stand
before the same great mystery, and the world's
welfare seems swaying in the balance of a man's
will. How the Most High can leave men free to
choose, and how He can hear and answer prayers,
as if He were a man that could repent; these are
questions higher than heaven, deeper than hell,
and the answer to them, if even the angels can give
it, reaches not down to us here below. · But shall
we, because we cannot understand prayer, resolve

to cease from it? It would be as difficult for us to shut out prayer altogether, as it would be to forbid the action of the human will. For every nation has felt the instinct to worship. Not only in the holy name of Christ have prayers been offered, but in the names of those that were no gods; nay, even "the unknown god" has not been without an altar. Ever in its peril and distress the human heart leaps forward as by an instinct to clasp the outstretched arm of the God of succour, believed in then though unseen. Where the dismasted ship is heaving and drifting over the pitiless stormy sea, there, in the midst of the last anguish, voices are heard calling on God with a fervour perhaps which they never knew before. At the sick-bedside, when art has done its utmost, and hope is almost gone, affection finds that it has no other outlet save in prayer. When the springs of life wax weak within us, or some prop on which we leaned has suddenly failed us, we do no violence to our nature, we only obey it, if we lift up our thoughts to Him who alone sits above the water-floods, unchangeable for ever. God, who has planted this instinct in us Himself, must surely know the way to answer it. When we urge the Omnipotent with our prayers, we do not derogate

from His right to govern the world without appeal; we only do as He has taught us, and leave
the results to Him to harmonise. It is no more
an error to pray than it is to see or to hear; in all
these things we are acting as He has made us.
Let us admit, then, that prayer is a mystery; that
it brings us close to the nature of God our Father,
whom our eyes cannot see nor our reason compass.
Yet let us pray on, more and more frequently,
and we shall know that we are not unheard. We
shall say from our own experience, "In my distress I called upon the Lord, and cried to my
God: he heard my voice out of his holy temple,
and my cry did enter into his ears," (2 Sam.
xxii. 7.)

2. Prayer, then, is natural. And yet the scriptural prayer is far from easy. For what does that
phrase, "Asking in the name of Christ," really
mean? It implies two things, an earnest belief
in the power and presence of Christ, and a sense of
the mind of Christ which shall teach the worshipper what to ask from his heavenly Father.
In other words, prayer must be first *earnest*, and
next *right-minded*.

a. Earnest prayer is not easy. It is told of
Anselm that, as he was walking with a friend, they

saw a boy tormenting a bird by letting it fly upwards towards the heavens, in which it would fain
ride and hover, and pulling it back again after each
flight by a thread fastened to its foot. "Our soul,"
said Anselm, "is like that bird. The spirit is
willing, but the flesh is weak. Our souls, weary
with sin, would fain fly upward and escape, but
there is the thread to our foot to pull us back
again. Earthly luxury and avarice cleave to us;
the needs and instincts of our earthly life cut short
our flight, and bring us back to the earth again,
unless God's grace set us free, as I free this bird."[*]
It needed not perhaps this apt parable to prove to
any one that it is very hard to pray in earnest. If
a husband were condemned to die, and a wife
could find her way to the foot of a throne where
lay the power of life and death, we can imagine
with what earnestness she would plead for his
pardon, how, if words failed, tears, and the agony
working in her face, would be eloquent in begging
the boon of a beloved life. And when a man
enters into his closet, and shuts the door, to pray,
there again is the King, present, looking, listening;
there is the soul in peril, and there is one that
should plead for himself and for all that he loves.

[*] Eadmer *de Anselmi Similitudinibus*, ch. 190.

But the tongue is slow, and the emotions dull and languid, and the whole transaction too often an unreality striving to be real. It is hard to pray in the name and power of Christ. He was present, but we could not fully believe it ; He would have heard, not merely spoken words, but the thought, the half-formed wish of the heart. The need was real, terribly real ; there is not a day that we do not feel it. Temptations find us weak ; losses and sorrows pursue us; and the very tenure of our life is so frail, that we know it may at any moment break under our feet, and let us sink into the deep water. And yet we find it hard to pray ! *Does* not that prove to us that our belief in our own act is not thoroughly sincere ? We only half believe that whatever we ask, the Father will give us in the name of the Son, and that in our closet thère are verily present a feeling heart to answer to the wishes of our heart, and an eye to see our wants, and an ear to listen to their expression. We know not how near a hearty prayer can bring us to the throne of the Father, where the Son, divine and human, sits on His right hand. We pray, yet doubt about prayer. We try to fly upward, but the thread round our foot draws us down to the earth again. .

b. Nor is it easy, in the second place, to pray with the mind of Christ—to seek such things only as are pleasing to Him. The words of my text seem indeed to warrant every kind of request. " *Whatsoever* ye shall ask the Father in my name he will give it'you." But those short words, " In my name," raise up a great barrier against all selfish worldly importunity. Two of those very disciples to whom Jesus spoke had asked for places of honour in His future kingdom. It was a self-seeking request ; it was one with which His name, His spirit, could have nothing to do. And He repelled their petition. " Ye know not what ye ask," (Mark x. 38.) Our Lord's promise is addressed to those who were about to receive His Spirit, and by that Spirit to be fashioned inwardly in His likeness, to learn His mind and will, to love what He loves, and hate what displeases Him. And the promise is, that all that they should ask in His name—that is, according to the usage of the Bible, in His power and Spirit—should be granted them. Now, the first effect of the presence of the Spirit in them would be to hinder all profane and selfish petitions. When Christians pray, God in them speaks to God in heaven. Their prayer is like the moisture of the earth ascending again into the firmament, whence it had lately descended in refreshing rain. Not from the lips of one in whom that *S*pirit is can come the request to be made great, or rich, or wise of head, or eloquent of speech ; not from him the wish to be avenged of his enemies ; because the divine *S*pirit within him is not a spirit of honour, or wealth, or enjoyment, or revenge, but the spirit of holiness and of the fear of God. And every prayer that savours of selfishness is not offered, cannot be offered, in the name of Christ. It is the voice of our own desires rudely breaking in upon the utterance of the better spirit. Never in this life shall the *full* force of our blessed Lord's promise be realised even by those chosen disciples. Never shall they feel the full joy of being seen and visited by Him, of utter freedom from all doubt, of being able to ask in His name without fear of asking amiss, until death shall have broken down the last barrier between them and their Master, until there shall be nothing between their souls and the fiery light of the Sun of Righteousness. All that they shall then ask of Him will be that He will give them more light and more life, and draw up their spirit more and more into His own. Other wants they shall feel no longer; and hardly can that be called a want which is supplied in the very moment of asking.

Is this promise, then, of no effect to those who must struggle on earth with trial and temptation? Did our Lord intend to console the disciples only by the promise of joy and security afar off, and to hide from them all the arduous life between? Not so. The life of the soul, and all the promises of God about it, unfold themselves gradually, like the life of a plant. It is quite consistent to say that these words have their *perfect* fulfilment for the disciples in another life, and at the same time that they began to be fulfilled after the resurrection. Then He did see them again, but occasionally, and with awe on their side and reserve on His. Then did they ask of the Father in His name, but doubtfully, or even wrongly, for the light of the Spirit was not yet. After the day of Pentecost the words advanced one degree nearer their fulfilment. The Spirit of Christ saw them, and caused them to rejoice; and it was hard even for their persecutors to take from them their joy; and they were taught what to ask of God, and they found that He gave them more abundantly than they asked. But even

then the true disciple had his seasons of darkness
and heaviness, when the sense of trust in God became weak and the words of prayer would not be
uttered, or when spurious desires mingled with holy
prayers, and the man prayed for power or honour,
under the specious hope that so he could do God
greater service. Yes; the soul needs an education
in prayer—grows and waxes strong in prayer ; and
the prayers of the man are a gauge of his whole
spiritual state. He is able to offer them in the
name of Christ—in the spirit and power of Christ
—from the first moment of real belief in Him.
But as he learns more fully what Christ would
have him do, his prayers grow stronger and prevail
more. The lisping syllables of a child are not
more distant from the eloquence that carries every
heart along with it than are the raw prayers of one
new born to Christ from the worship of a just man
made perfect. Let not our hearts be troubled over-
much that we cannot pray as we ought ; let us try
to *grow* in prayer, let us pray most for the gift of
prayer. All good men who have laid their inner
experience open to the world have confessed that
this very short-coming which we deplore was also
theirs. The prayer that can wrest a blessing from
God, the knocking that shall instantly be opened

to, are not for the beginning but the completeness of Christian life.

3. But we are too apt to associate prayer exclusively with the house of God, or with the knees bended at the bedside in the silence of the night, and to separate it from the trials and business of life. Now, it is not every one who can find time for long and frequent communing in secret with God; but every one can lead a praying life. "I have much ado to pray," says Luther, "and when I have said the Lord's Prayer and thought on one or two passages of Scripture, I lay me down and sleep."* Yet ever out of the warfare of that stormy life of his rose up the incense of prayer to God most High. Every day of it proclaimed that *there* was a man to whom God was a strong rock and house of defence, whose wish it was to live for God, and to be afraid of no man's face whilst God was with him. Far better it is to live so than to lengthen out the morning and evening orisons with many words, and give the day and all its actions up to greed, and sensuality, and sluggishness. It is best of all to be able so to command our time as to give to active duty and to secret prayer their due proportion. But the most active can pray to

* *Table-Talk.*

God, and turn his very activity into a prayer. To carry through every action as a holy work, seen of God and judged by Him, this is to lead a life of prayer. A sudden temptation befalls us; and the fervent wish for a strength beyond our own to meet it flies up then and there to our God and Judge. A disappointment or a loss falls heavily on us; and amidst our distress we are able to say, It is the Lord; let Him do what seemeth Him good. Some one most dear to us goes forth from our hearth to face the world's trials; and a heartfelt word commends him to God, who alone is able to keep him safe to the end. Our temper, our industry, our resolutions for good, do not keep pace with our wishes. We hate and abhor the shortcoming, and wish that God's love might possess us wholly, and burn out of us all baser feelings. Such occasions are the stuff of which our human life is made up; and every one of them may become an acted prayer to God. It is for this daily battle that the promise of our Lord is unspeakably precious to us. "Ask, and ye shall receive, that your joy may be full," (John xvi. 24.) The prayer may be short; but if it come hot from the heart of one in the thick of the battle, will it not reach the ear to which it is sent? A few words—Lord, save us! we

perish—roused up the Redeemer to save His disciples from the devouring sea. Ah! these prayers
of men that struggle are dear to Him that hears
them; they consecrate a life, they make a man's
heart a very church or temple in which worship is
continually offered. These are not days when the
more useful minds can find leisure for much retire-
ment and self-communing. But to carry the praying heart about with us into all that our hands find
to do is the special need of our time.

Let us pray, then, that God will give us the spirit
of prayer, without which no will is brave, no brain
wise, no fortune secure; that He will aid us to overcome those earthly inclinations which make our
prayers faint and half-hearted; that He will cause
us to remember Him in the sudden temptation or
sorrow, and give us the wish to flee to Him for
succour; that He will show us ever deeper and
deeper truth in the divine promise in my text.
And may He make us long more and more to do
His will! "As the hart panteth after the water-
brooks, so panteth my soul after thee, O God.
Why art thou cast down, O my soul? and why
art thou disquieted in me? Hope thou in God:
for I shall yet praise him for the help of his
countenance," (Ps. xlii. 1, 5.)

XI.

MIRACLES.

PREACHED BEFORE THE UNIVERSITY OF OXFORD, 1865.

"Jesus went about all Galilee, teaching in their synagogues, and preaching the gospel of the kingdom, and healing all manner of sickness and all manner of disease among the people." .

THE Son of man went about Galilee to preach and to heal. Not alone to preach, to such a race of people, words which they would care for so little; but to confirm the teaching with signs following. Not alone to work wonders that men might fall down to Him in fear; but to teach His great message of deliverance, whilst He showed at the same time an unusual power to deliver. Nor is this passage an isolated testimony to this fact. The place which miracles hold in the history of the Redeemer is that of a close co-ordination and connexion between them and His doctrine and His person. His character, His doctrine, His wonder-working power, are all witnesses together of His divine nature, power, and commission.

N

The notion of miracles that has sometimes found its way into popular theology—namely, that they are certain proofs or credentials by which the divine Ambassador proved His commission from God, which, but for these tokens, would have lacked proof, has scarcely any plausible ground from Holy Scripture. If it be supposed that the teaching of Jesus required, as a condition precedent to its being believed, the performance of some wonder in order to prove that the Teacher was divine, then what becomes of the evidence which the teaching itself furnished? " When Jesus had ended these sayings, the people were astonished at his *doctrine*," (Matt. vii. 28.) Or if there must be the precedent condition of a miraculous surprise before a disciple could cleave with love to his new-found Lord, whose words of wisdom and love attracted him, our conception of the Lord's character must be lower than that which we attribute even to merely human teachers and friends; who gather to themselves the fruit of the hearts and affections of men, without needing to prove beforehand that they are worthy. The stamp of the divine seal is on all three, on doctrine, on life, and on marvellous works. It could not be admitted that miracles made credible a doctrine

which otherwise failed to manifest itself as
divine; or made notable a character which otherwise would have passed without censure and admiration alike. No; the cord of faith which
binds men to the Lord of Glory is of three
strands ; it is twisted of example, word, and work.
It may be that in the earliest age, the thread of
work bore the greatest strain, and miracles were
needed first of all to get a hearing for that strange
doctrine, and attract an eye to that obscure life.
It may be that somewhat later the strand of
doctrine had to resist the most, the strain of many
philosophies, and many heathen political institutions, before Christ's message of sin and forgiveness and the cross could settle into its place in
hearts that believed it, in political systems that
found it good. It may be that later still, when
miracles were no longer seen wonders, but facts
of history, when the doctrine of self-denial in
Christ the self-denier had triumphed for ever
over gnostic fancies and stoic endurance, and
epicurean schemes of delight, the example of
Jesus, the contemplation of His sinless life, is the
element that binds us to Him most firmly. But
it is not for us to unwind this threefold cord
of love. Christ is not a worker of prodigies: He

is the eternal Son of God, speaking the things which His Father had told Him, and working with the same power as that with which His Father worketh. And when we are invited to discuss the subject of miracles by itself, apart from the person of the worker, and the message which He came to bring, we abandon on the one hand the position in which the miracles stand in the Bible, and we lay ourselves open on the other hand to objections, some urged in the interest of physical science, and others in that of historical criticism, which would have had no power at all against us so long as we stood upon scriptural ground.

Remark then, in the first place, how closely related miracles are to the person of the doer in the scriptural representations. They are called mighty works, signs, wonders. Once only those who see them call them strange things, παράδοξα, things which none could have looked for. But this only expresses the first astonishment of by-standers; it is not the word of the Lord or of the Evangelist. Now, of the usual names, only one refers to the effect of astonishment upon the beholders; *i.e.*, wonders. But it is remarkable that, when this name is used, another is usually added. "Except ye see signs and wonders, ye will not believe," (John iv. 48.) The other names have relation to the doer and to His mission. Mighty works : these are signs of the doer's power. Signs : these are tokens that the Messiah is here ; for the prophets of the old covenant taught the Jews to look for such tokens in any one that professed to be the Prophet sent of God. To say the least, there is a very great preponderance of places where miracles are described as tokens of the power and position of the Redeemer, over those where they are mentioned in their mere power to astonish the beholder and strike him with fear and conviction.

Remark, in the next place, how the very nature of the miracles connects them inseparably with the doer of them. Almost every one of them goes directly to show Jesus as a loving and compassionate friend of sinful men. Every degree of human need, from Lazarus now returning to dust, from the palsy that has seized on brain and nerves, and is, so to speak, a death in life, from the leprosy which tainted every drop in the veins with a poison of which the loathsome skin was only a token, up to the injury to a particular limb or the faintness from want of accustomed food, received succour from the powerful word of Christ ; with whom it was neither more nor less difficult to wrest His buried friend from corruption and the worm, than to heal a withered hand or restore to its place an ear that had been cut off. When the savage demoniac, wandering naked among the rock-tombs of the Gadarenes, is turned into a sound man, "sitting, and clothed, and in his right mind," (Mark v..15,) it is only such as the Gadarenes, who could see in this anything short of a great manifestation of divine love. When the Syro-Phœnician mother, importunate that her afflicted daughter should share some of the blessings which Jesus had been showering on the children of Israel, even with no better claim than that of the dog picking up the crumbs from the master's table, receives her dearest wish, she cannot fail to look for ever on Him who had done this marvellous work as divine in power, divine in love, and human in His sympathy with sorrow. He, and not the surprising cure, will occupy the field of her memory. And in those works where the power of God is more manifest than the love, as in that case where the divine agency comes in for no higher object than to furnish wine for the marriage feast, the minds of the witnesses are meant to be drawn to Him by the miracle, as to one able even to *create* the food that

God alone can give for the sustenance of men.
Christ is love—Christ is the power of God : these
are the tones which are heard in every one of those
wonderful works. He came not to amaze men,
but to attract them ; to draw them to Himself out
of the ways of sin. The miracles are part of the
garb of glory wherewith He is clothed. Under
that garb Christ Himself moved ; and men were
not to admire its brightness and its wonderful
texture, but to say, Behold, here is Christ. This
is the Son of *David*, the *Saviour* of the world, the
leader of His people. He did the miracles, and
thereby manifested forth His glory, and His disciples believed on Him, (John ii. 11.)

Let us remark further, that if the object of the
miracles were to challenge submission of the
mind to a new doctrine by means of mere awe
and wonder, it would be impossible to understand
why faith in Christ should be made the condition
of receiving miraculous help. The most obstinate
unbeliever would be the best subject for a miracle,
if the purpose of a miracle were to force belief.
If the end is gained when men are astonished and
put to silence by marvels too striking to resist,
then seek not the half-believers for witnesses, for
they are already almost gained. Seek the place

rather where *S*cribe and Pharisee and chief-priest
are gathered most thickly together, with hearts
hardened against all evidence. There, if the Lord
from the pinnacle above the porch of the Temple,
that overhangs the deep valley, shall cast Himself
down the dizzy height of porch and precipice, and
depart alive, every heart will admit that there is
power. *S*ome may whisper " Through Beelzebub
—through Beelzebub:" but at least all will listen
now, and all will fear to plot His betrayal or to
seek to hurt Him. Nay, some great sign from
heaven may strike down a whole nation into
assent. *S*ome fiery pillar to hover about this
heavenly wanderer's halting-place at night, or
some pillar of cloud to go before His face by day;
these will be seen by thousands, and bruited about
through every corner of Galilee and Jewry, until
every child can tell the tale of a supernatural
presence visibly attesting Jesus of Nazareth.
None of these things takes place. It is plain
that mere astonishment at miracles was not the
object of the Lord. For He turns not to the
most unbelieving, but to those whose hearts are
given over to Him wholly or in part already. He
makes faith in Him the condition of His succour.
"Believest thou that I can do this?" "Lord, if

thou wilt, thou canst make me clean. . . . I will; be thou clean," (Matt. viii. 2, 3.) "If thou canst believe, all things are possible to him that believeth. . . . Lord, I believe; help thou mine unbelief," (Mark ix. 23, 24.) In all these cases, the faith that Jesus must awake, the faith that is put forth unasked, the faith that falters, mixed with unbelief, are sufficient passports to His ͺloving help. But this demand of belief as a condition of doing works which were themselves to produce belief, throws a great light upon the nature of miracles. To him that hath shall be given. The one great purpose of the Lord was to draw men's souls to Him that they might be saved; and they must be drawn, not through terror, but by their will. Hearts broken by trouble of some passing kind bethink them that with Jesus there may be deliverance. These, who are taking the first step towards Him, drawn by the thread of a love, of a belief, which they themselves do not half understand, He will take, and will not only deliver them from the present suffering, but will open to them a greater depth of suffering and a far greater power of deliverance in their sin and in His redemption. Study in this light the account of. the paralytic at the pool of Bethesda. "Wilt thou be made whole? . . . Behold, thou art made whole: sin no more, lest a worse thing come unto thee," (John v. 6, 14.) It is as though He said, "Thou hast chosen thy present state; dost thou choose deliverance?" And then when He finds him in the Temple, come there, we may think, in his newly-wakened faith to give thanks to God, He reminds him that sin had caused his ailment, and that he must flee from that and from the shadow of a coming wrath against that. It was a mercy to those who had begun to believe, to fan with the breath of love their little spark of love into an abiding fire. On the other side, it was a mercy less easy to be understood, yet still a mercy, not to force upon the hardened, wonders which they would still blaspheme. To multiply proofs of divine power in the eyes of those who had hardened themselves against all proof, would only deepen their condemnation. "If I had not done among them the works which none other man did, they had not had sin: but now have they both seen and hated both me and my Father," (John xv. 24.) He could not offer Himself to them that would receive Him without being by some rejected; it is in the nature of a trial and a choice that some should be able to refuse. But every one who heard the gospel message, and saw it confirmed with signs, and yet rejected it, was the worse for his opportunity: he had now seen and hated both Christ and the Father. And therefore the merciful Lord, lest they should add sin to sin, refrained from works where none believed. The plains of Galilee saw more of His wonders than the streets of Jerusalem, and the crowd of simple peasants ate miraculous bread which He never created for the hardened priest and Pharisee ; and He raised to life not the dead of Jerusalem, but of Nain, of Bethany, of Capernaum ; and he preferred to work wonders not in towns, where men of all sorts were gathered thick together, but on mountain and seashore and in quiet places, where men gathered of their own will to see and hear Him.

Very significant, too, are those charges to tell no man, to let no man know the miracle, which are so often addressed to the witnesses of it. They are quite beyond comprehension on the view that the object of miracles was to astonish and overawe men's minds, without reference to a right conception of the doer of them. Had this been the divine purpose, some great work done upon some public gathering in Jerusalem might have been

witnessed by thousands, who would have filled
with the rumour of it every corner of the country.
Every town and village might have known, before it
saw Him, the fame of the coming Lord, Wonder-
worker, King, and *Sage.* Every witness, be his
inward condition what it might, would have become
an apostle as to this point only, that Jesus had
dominion over the powers of nature. But I understand the injunction, if it be true that the knowledge of His Person, of His truth, was to go along
with the witness of His miracles. He will not be
known to the people whom He seeks, as rumour,
with its hundredfold distortions, would have re-
ported Him. He will be known as He is, as the
loving *Saviour* of men. Miracles are nothing in
themselves; they are to be viewed as tokens of
that higher light which has broken through into
the lower darkness of a ruined world. His wonders
shall not go forth by themselves, with all the false
glosses of excited reporters, all the exaggerations
and mistakes of those who would have their Master
to be like themselves. No; wherever the fame
of them shall come, He too shall come. In the
form of a servant, in fashion as a man, humbling
Himself for the sake of men, and ready to be
obedient unto death, even the death of the cross.

Wherever the miracles are bruited the doctrine of the Lord shall also be known—the chastening doctrine which brings all under sin, and tells us that there is a sorrow deeper than sorrow, and a blindness and a lameness worse than those which Jesus healed with a word, and which turns our eyes to Him as the healer of that worst sorrow, worst trouble, worst death, the being lost to God through the sin that is in us.

These elements being given, we should describe the miracles of the gospel as works done by Christ in the course of His divine mission of mercy, which could not have proceeded from ordinary causes then in operation, and therefore proved the presence of a superhuman power, and which, by their nature and drift, showed that this power was being exerted in the direction of love and compassion for the salvation of mankind.

Great consequences depend on a right view of miracles, whether these are viewed in the light of historical criticism or of natural science. Let me say a few words from each of these points of view.

If I were to avow that I could not establish the truth of the miracles taken by themselves, I should be entitled to add that the Bible never so presents them, that it is unnatural to discuss one class of acts of any great person, shutting out artificially all thought of his character and his position, which must needs throw some light upon the acts. I might add, too, that the miracles which were once watched with astonishment by eager eyes, and smote the mind with swift conviction, are for us distant historical facts, recorded by two or three writers only; and that if you doubt these, our resource lies only in scholarly discussion of the documents, and in arguments about the internal marks of truth which they bear. No fresh miracles can be called in to confirm the old; no witnesses examined in confirmation of the evangelists, if you venture to doubt them. And hence it is plausible to say, and difficult to refute, that between the miracles of the gospel, taken by themselves, and the marvels assigned to other agents, a clear boundary-line cannot be drawn. But we refuse to view them by themselves. Do you not see that lapse of time has changed their relation to Christ? Once men knew not Christ; but they saw His works, and believed Him for the works' sake. Once miracles were needed to mark out Christ the Lord; now Christ attests to us the miracles. The Jews said, We see these wonders done; therefore the doer is the Son of God. The Christian at present says, We see

that Christ is the Son of God ; therefore miracles
and mighty works were likely to be showed forth
by Him. And this is no distinction of bare logic :
it is all-important. To us the great assurance that
the gospel story is a true one is, that Christ is in
that record, of a beauty and a worth such as no
man invented, a picture coloured as no human
limner ever could draw, luminous with tints of
heaven. Whence came this story ? written in
what age ? how preserved ? Ah ! these matter not.
The Lord Himself is here, and is His own witness.
I sit down at His feet, and listen to His words.
He reads me the riddle of my existence ; tells of
the divine stamp and seal in man's nature, so per-
feet, so noble, were it not cast down and broken in
two. He opens out a hope of reparation ; so that
we shall not always be such weak and wayward
children, willing good, and unable to do it, admiring the law of holiness, but unable to walk therein.
All the books upon my shelves fail to show me the
secrets of human nature half so well as these little
books do. Books they are, written amongst Jews
when that nation had lost faith in its destinies,
when its morals were debased, when its literature
was exhausted, when the days of its existence
as a nation were numbered. The writers of them,

whoever they are, have done that which no most cultivated philosopher, rich with traditions of past philosophies, and endowed with leisure and with free intercourse with the best and wisest, has ever approached to. More than this, the life of Jesus is even more miraculous to us than His teaching ; and that life these four books do one and all describe. Jesus is there, sinless Himself, yet merciful to sinners ; wielding great powers and professing great purposes, which are to affect all the world and all the coming ages, yet ever with a self-restraining humility, with a meekness under provocations, such as have never gone with great power before. Words would fail to sum up this character, without a parallel in history, combining, as it does, in perfect harmony, powers the most opposite. Here are meekness without feebleness, dignity without arrogance, purity, with a deep insight into the nature of evil, a lofty assertion of power, and a tenderness towards the humble. Is it our first assertion on reading the gospels, that some of the works of Christ are marvellous and hard to be believed ? No : first of all, Christ was marvellous, and came on earth for a wonderful purpose. If wonders are a burden to me, I cannot get rid of these wonders. But then, I shall be told, objec-

tions to the miracles will invalidate the witness of
the gospels, and so we shall be rid of all. No.
Two miracles remain, and defy you; the character of Christ, and the message of Christ. I saw
not the pen that wrote the account of them, nor
need I that proof that they are superhuman.
Some one wrote this gospel, and that one; whoever wrote them, describes the superhuman. We
can now survey the ages, and know the best that
man's invention can compass under the most
favourable conditions. The character of Jesus is
unlike all these inventions, and incomparably
above them. And therefore the historical question
is not whether miracles by themselves are probable, and whether we can admit them upon such
testimony as we have, but whether the Lord from
heaven, who lived on this earth—for none could
have invented the story of His life; who left a
message on earth—for none could have invented
that message; added to His utterances certain marvels of love and compassion to draw men's eyes towards Him for their good. It is not probable that
miracles should be done; but it is probable that a
Being, marked in every word and precept as a superhuman power, should be superhuman, as in His
inner worth so in His outward activity, as in His

O

teaching so in His doings towards the children of men.

Yet one word more upon the scientific objection to miracles. We are told that the phenomena of nature are so many links in a chain of causes and effects, and that to suppose that God breaks through this chain, which with all its cunning workmanship and strength He has formed, is to make God contradict Himself, and be at variance with Himself. We are told that such a phrase as "suspension of the laws of nature" is inadmissible; that the laws of the world are part of the world itself, and cannot be put aside. We are told that every year of scientific research adds confidence to the law of the uniformity of nature. To these let it be answered, that there are already, apart from any question of miracles, flaws in this chain of causation, or rather powers from without that can shake it. One of these is the existence of sin and evil. Were physical causes left to their own working, a given country would be fertile and prosperous. War breaks out, and that country is wasted : its best cities wrecked, its inhabitants oppressed by tributes and exactions till they are ruined. After a century or two have passed, it bears upon it still the scathing marks of man's.

evil will.* You will say, perhaps, that the wills of men are links in this unalterable chain of causation. Nay, but you punish them, you reward; you treat them as alterable, governable, amenable to your pressure. Be not, then, too jealous for a scheme of causation which after all you cannot guarantee from all apparent interference. If God, in the smooth working of the ordered universe, finds room for man's waywardness, if He has made room for the enormous influence which Christianity itself has had upon the world, then He could also find room for the miracles that attested its beginnings.

Then, as to the phrase "suspension of the laws of nature," be it remembered that holy Scripture is not responsible for this. Laws are not suspended; the forces always seek to operate, but they may be prevented by other laws from their operation at present. Thus some of the characters of animal life are that it assimilates matter for its sustenance, in the shape of food, and that it protects from the universal law of decay of organic matter the particles so assimilated, so long as they are part of its frame and needful for its functions. Suppose a world in which no animal life had yet existed, and

* See page 179.

introduce into it by some preternatural means a completely organised animal. The vegetable food that this animal eats is exempted from its fate as marked down for it in the existing law of causation; it ought to have withered away like grass, and been dissipated and re-embodied in other plants, or in the soil where it fell. It is now subject to all the marvellous phenomena of life. It ministers to unheard-of powers and functions, motion, sight, strength to destroy, and the like. And in one sense this might be regarded as a case in which the laws of nature were suspended. But any one who knew that it was an untimely first-fruit of a great animal system, soon to be created, would rather conceive it as a glimpse into a new group of laws and operations hereafter to be seen more fully. And this we conceive the miracles to have been. We do not dogmatise about their nature; we only caution science not to be over zealous for the inviolability of laws, the outside limits of which she cannot now ascertain. There is at least nothing contrary to science in the belief that a time might come when a great yearning of compassion might as a rule achieve the cure it desired to see; when the bidding of a will, strong in good, might exorcise what remained of evil in some

weaker will. Not here and now; but we know
that the spiritual kingdom will not always be so
weak, and the scattered bands of Satan's army,
which Christ by His victory broke up, be still so
strong to harass us. Then casting ourselves with
a complete abandonment upon the bosom of
a seen Saviour, and compassed about with the
felt arms of His protection, we may be conscious
of changes, and a might, and a transformation
within us, that will show us that He is God indeed.
Then we may know that behind the facts and
phenomena which our short reach can compass
and our weak eyes observe, other and greater
facts lay hid. Through an occasional rift in the
cloudy atmosphere God showed us them; and we
were jealous lest they should fly out and be ex-
ceptions from an order that seemed so fixed.
But they are only part of the great chain of laws
and causes, to which all facts spiritual and natural
belong; only they are brighter links, for they are
nearer to the great hand that holds them on high,
and larger, for they have more to bear. Miracles
are but part of the gospel; we will judge them in
the setting where they are placed. Those who
received them at first were not made Christian by
them; there was a germ of faith which came from

knowing Christ as well as what He did. To us they are not even the beginning of faith; for Christ was our household teacher and friend before our unripe minds could conceive what miracles meant. He, the sinless Lord, is our first miracle; His teaching of sin and holiness and redemption is our second miracle; if you ask a third, it is the transforming power of the gospel in human hearts. Turn your acuteness and your reasoning first to these. *Do* not insulate the miracles from these, with which the *S*criptures knit them up so closely, and then pretend that the evidence is insufficient when you have yourself struck out nine-tenths of it. Before Christ's works, know Christ. He says Himself, "I, if I be lifted up from the earth, will draw all men unto me," (John xii. 32.) There is that power of attraction in His life, lessons, and works. Those who accept this threefold witness, will feel the power of His own invitation, "Come unto me, all ye that labour and are heavy laden, and I will give you rest. Take my yoke upon you, and learn of me ; for I am meek and lowly in heart : and ye shall find rest unto your souls. For my yoke is easy, and my burden is light," (Matt. xi. 28–30.)

XII.

THE INTERCEDING SPIRIT.

PREACHED BEFORE THE UNIVERSITY OF OXFORD,
WHITSUNDAY, 1867.

" For we know that the whole creation groaneth and travaileth in pain together until now : and not only they, but ourselves also, which have the firstfruits of the Spirit, even we ourselves groan within ourselves, waiting for the adoption, to wit, the redemption of our body. For we are saved by hope : but hope that is seen is not hope : for what a man seeth, why doth he yet hope for ? But if we hope for that we see not, then do we with patience wait for it. Likewise the Spirit also helpeth our infirmities : for we know not what we should pray for as we ought : but the Spirit itself maketh intercession for us with groanings which cannot be uttered. And he that searcheth the hearts knoweth what is the mind of the Spirit, because he maketh intercession for the saints according to the will of God."

THAT the state of the Church, even when the Holy Spirit was manifestly present in it as its life, was a state of struggle and aspiration, is confessed in these great words, and nowhere else with the like force. Creation had long groaned in the throes of its deliverance. But even after deliverance granted, after the life-giving Spirit was sent, the deliverance was not complete. There were the firstfruits, but not the complete ingathering. There was the adoption of. sons, but not that

complete sonship, when the body shall be redeemed from sin and passion. There was the
hope of salvation, but not the open vision of it.
To wait with patience for what was yet to come
was the lot and the wisdom of the saints of God ;
yes, even of one like Paul, sure of his calling, sure
that the Spirit was with him, with a vigorous faith
holding still upon God, as a strong man's hand
grasps his sword in danger. Paul could confess, as
we are fain to do, that hope, and waiting, and imperfect light, and a hard struggle, are the portion
of the people of God. Nay, the Spirit of God, the
Comforter promised of Christ, is spoken of as helping our weakness. So weak are we that we cannot
even pray rightly ; and the Spirit of God, and no
less an advocate, intercedes for us with groanings
that cannot be described or uttered. But whilst
we hardly know the meaning of our own aspirations, God knows it, because the pleading of the
Spirit in us is according to His mind and will, and
He reads in our hearts the longing and the yearning which we could never express fully to Him.
This picture of the Spirit, as it were in His humiliation, has been quoted in old times to countenance the theory that He was less than God the
Father. But as Jesus hungered and wept, and

offered His suffering body on the altar of the cross, and yet was still the Lord of glory, so does the Spirit, dwelling in our flesh, with the darkness of it, and the weakness, and the perversity, plead for us with groanings that cannot be uttered, and strengthen our weak hand and sustain our flagging hope ; and yet He is still the Comforter, the Spirit of truth sent from the Father by the Son, to be to the disciples the sufficient substitute of their ascended Lord.

But it is rather for their practical importance than for their bearing on the mystery of the divine nature that these words are precious to us. When that miracle of Pentecost turned back the tide of affliction from Christ's disciples, and promised them triumph instead of defeat, and showed them God fighting on their side instead of man exulting against them, amidst the tumult of feelings then awakened there must have been a great feeling of security and triumph, a sense that their deliverance was complete. Patience yet awhile ! The travail-pains of the earth that have so long continued are not yet over ! Every day shows it. Ananias tells his lie in the midst of us. Apostles quarrel and go asunder. The spiritual life of churches is weak, and needs encouragement,

advice, and rebuke. You might almost be brought
to say that here and there the Spirit had ceased to
lighten and to comfort. For man's hopes outstrip
the redemption which man himself hinders in its
working. He will have at once the glorious Church
without spot or wrinkle, but he will not cease to
stain it with his own sins. The Church shall be a
vessel of gold, worthy to hold the treasure of the
Spirit; but the breath of man's own anger and
passion tarnishes the beaten surface. And the
Spirit of God, completing the work of love which
Christ stooped to accomplish, humiliates Himself
to the level of this imperfect creature, so wildly
demanding to be served with perfect things ; and
because man knows not even that first step of
holiness, to pray for right things as he ought, the
Spirit kneels with him and shapes for him words of
prayer too great for him to understand completely.
The Spirit puts a hand to the pressing burden of
his infirmity, and eases his weary shoulder of it.
The kingdom of heaven has come indeed, and the
Spirit of God is present there ; but its watchwords
still are faith, and expectation, and endurance·
And the greater glory, the thrones for those who
have triumphed round the great throne of Him
that triumphed first, the kingdom where tears are

not, for God has wiped them, where darkness is not, for the Lord God is the Sun and the Light of it, these are still to come. Oh, great condescension of God, by which we are taught to know Him! We know Christ, condescending to the cross for our sins; now, we must know the Spirit of God, kneeling with us and supplying strange strength to our uplifted hands. He joins in prayers, and in such poor blind prayers; He enters into and dwells in a soul wasted in worldly thoughts and passions.

Now, I will not attempt to vindicate once more the theological doctrine of the presence of the Holy Spirit; I will only ask, What does this doctrine amount to when translated into the language of our modern wants? I will seek from it what comfort can be found for those young minds who, at this time more perhaps than at another, are in need of some sure support.

a. At a time when many insist on explaining all the facts of the universe by material laws, what is it that gives us an assurance that there is something in us which is not subject to the conditions of matter? It is the fact that we can will—can choose. Without freedom of will there is no such thing as obedience, and obedience to the law of duty is the highest calling of man. The more

complete the freedom the more perfect the obedience can be. He who is not free may bend, may
submit, may be compelled; but obey, in the true
sense of that word, he cannot. We know the
death of the moral nature by discovering that the
power of choosing is lost to us. "To will is present with me; but how to perform that which I
will I find not," (Rom. vii. 18.) Well may St Paul
describe the man under the law by whom this can
be said as under a kind of death. "Who shall deliver me from the body of this death?" (ver. 24.)
For we know that our obedience to God must not
be the mere submission of the weak to the strong,
of the senseless man to the wise-directing mind.
We must not obey Him as rock, and stone, and
tree obey Him, revolving as He bids them with the
great world of which they are a part. We wish to
be able to see that His counsels are wise and good,
and to obey them because they are good, and to
have within us no rebellious thought to drag back
our willing feet when we would walk in the way of
His commandments. But this freedom is not possible so long as we continue in sin. We know it is
not possible. It is not that angels, wiser than we,
look down on us, and pity our self-deceit. We are
prompt to judge ourselves in this. "Who shall

deliver us from the body of this death?" There
comes across us some bright gleam of God's truth,
or a moment of remorse, or a generous impulse
to emulate the great and the good. But our self-
experience refutes these new convictions. Other
impulses like them have been ours before; but the
corruption in us was too strong for them. Why
stand admiring the brightness of the truth? Why
trust the noble impulses? Other gleams as bright
have gone out into thick darkness, and we are what
we are. Chained in the prison of fleshly evil, the
soul looks out, with enough life in it to know that
there *is* light, and that true freedom is conceivable.
Who shall free her from her prison? Who shall
deliver her from the body of this death? Let St
Paul answer his own words. "The law of the
Spirit of life in Christ Jesus hath made me free
from the law of sin and death," (Rom. viii. 2.)
Something there is in them that believe which is a
law, and so asks for obedience, which is a spirit,
helping the infirmities of their spirit, which is life,
and therefore banishes this miserable feeling of
moral death, which is life in Christ Jesus, because
it comes from Him and leads them to Him. "If
Christ be in you, the body is dead because of sin;
but the Spirit is life because of righteousness," (ver.

10.)   So then this doctrine of the Spirit of God indwelling in them that believe is not an abstract dogma, but the very foundation of Christian morals.   To believe that the spark of hope, and faith, and good resolution, which we feel new-born in us, is God indeed working in us, is to be strong to act.   Past failures do not cause us to despair; the sin that is within us is a sin that must give way to One stronger than sin.   God is within us of a truth; and we feel that nothing can be against us. We feel free; and, in a sense, to feel freedom is to *be* free.

Yet can this be God working within us? Moments of strong prayer, passing into mere wandering and repetition of words after a time by reason of our infirmity of purpose; earnest resolutions to lean on Christ and love Him always, that are forgotten soon after they are made; our mixed thoughts, woven in the loom of the mind, a golden woof across the sordid warp of our old nature, can these broken efforts and scanty results be the power of Christ and of His Spirit?   Oh! not for us are these doubts, for the humiliation which causes them is for our sake.   So might the disciples have doubted the Lord Himself, because He suffered them to hunger and hungered with.

them; because scorn and death prevailed against Him. The Spirit that is in us leading us to good is divine, because it leads to good. Who are we that we doubt it because it is not enough? Who told us to expect that it should burn as fire all the old stubble of our souls, and leave us from the first moment pure and complete? Who has even assured us that this would be best for us? No; our own spirit kneels low in the humiliation that befits it, not knowing what to pray for as it ought; and the Spirit descending, kneels—(may I say so?) —beside it, humiliating Himself that we may be lifted up. Whence that Spirit comes we cannot doubt. Nowhere except from heaven can come this gentle comfort, these pure hopes, this turning from sin with abhorrence. Though the beginnings be small, they are yet divine. We walk but slowly, and we stumble; but we walk towards God, and God within us is the light of our path and the strength of our feet.

b. As with the work in our souls so with the work of God in His Church. There is not one age, not even the earliest, of the Church's history, in which we do not at the same time see that the Spirit is truly there with power and blessing, and that the work is less than we could wish it, the as-

P

pirations feebler, the adverse influences permitted too great a play. There is no greater trial of faith to thinking men than to study those tokens of apparent failure which the history of the Church everywhere presents. Lo! at the day of Pentecost the gates of heaven are open, and in power and wisdom God the Spirit descends upon His Church. Let Satan, with his cohorts of armed sins, roll back in confusion before the soldiers of God, heroic in their preternatural strength. Nor shall the army of evil ever reconquer any battlefield whereon the standard of the Lord has ever been planted. Proclaim it to all the ends of the world that the victory is won, and the King of Glory has come back to rule in peace the world that He has loved so much, yet so much suffered to stray. Shall there be left, after a decade or two, one single country in the broad world wherefrom the evil shall not have been cast out? This is the tone in which we would write Church history if truth would suffer us. And to write it as it was is hard indeed. We scarcely know how to record man's perversity without accusing the Lord of want of power to save. But as with the man so with the Church or nation, the Spirit has been an indwelling germ of life, and not an overruling and transforming omnipotence, suddenly expelling the old nature and making all things new. As with the man so with the Church, the Spirit has led and not compelled. Grace and strength sufficient for us have been always given. If we look on the countries of Christendom, if we examine the strange troubles and distractions to which any one is exposed who in this country and Church would seek guidance for his soul in the way of truth, we are tempted to question whether such results can ever be harmonised with such promises. What can there have been in Tyre and Sidon of luxury and passionate self-indulgence that Paris and London have not outdone? If the Pharisees of the first century despised and neglected the people whom they misled, is there nothing of that same spirit in us, in the way we look upon our untaught and misguided poor? Is there amongst us none of that pride of half-knowledge which St Paul condemned in the heathen philosophers? To worship the creature more than the Creator, is that a vice unknown in Christian lands? No. Nature and humanity are set up for a kind of worship, against religion ; and I wish we could say that religion herself had escaped this material taint. And yet these fallings-off are man's doing, not the doing of

the Spirit, Lord and Giver of life. As out of the
poor, perplexed soul of a man groanings that
cannot be expressed, the promptings of that Spirit
that will not leave him to himself, but will rather
share his humiliation, so out of the Churches and
the nations, be they never so distracted, rise the
same unspeakable prayers and yearnings after the
holy and the true. And whatever be the forms of
thought or philosophy that surround us, we are not
their slaves ; there is amongst us the true principle
of liberty, the Holy Spirit to teach us and to guide.
There still remain three great witnesses for redemption ; God speaking in His Word, and man's
conscience of sin, and the interceding Spirit trying
to bring him back to God. We are tempted sometimes to speak as though a young man's mind, or
an older mind, must needs be fashioned upon the
mould of those that are placed around him. God
forbid that this should be ! The spark of regene-
rative life burns still. The soul may turn and live.
The college clique or circle may cast out its wantonness, or its gambling, or its idleness. The nation
may undergo a purifying change; and this must be
from the means within it now, for God has given
His best gifts to us already. For a new Saviour,
or another Pentecost, or an enlarged New Testa-

ment, we shall look in vain. "From what quarter,"
says a foreign writer, "can healing come for the
apostasy of those who have had among them the
highest form and power of salvation, and forsaken
it? To the heathen world, when, like the prodigal,
it had spent its all, the Saviour came. But to
Christendom, when the space for repentance is
past, can He come only as Judge."*

c. The presence of the Comforter is not only a
reality, but it is better than the presence of Christ
Himself. We should not dare to say so, but Christ
has said it. "It is expedient for you that I go
away: for if I go not away, the Comforter will not
come unto you," (John xvi. 7.) These words put
on one side all notions that it is fanatical or super-
stitious to speak of the leading of the present Spirit
of God as the foundation of our moral freedom and
the source of all holiness. Why should it be fanatical? It is not fanatical to think that God exists
and sees, and thence to infer that all human life
and effort is from Him. "Except the Lord build
the house, they labour in vain that build it," (Ps.
cxxvii. 1.) It is not fanatical to believe that once,
upon a hill-side in Galilee, Jesus preached wise
words to them that would listen. And when He

---

* Thiersch, *Ch. Hist.*, p. 57.

tells them that He will go away and cease to teach
them, because He can send another instead of
Him, to warn, and teach, and remind, and convince,
and lead them, for this is better for them, where
is the new element that makes it fanaticism to believe this, if that was mere historical fact? Is it
that we can believe Christ because many saw Him,
and one even touched Him, but cannot believe the
*S*pirit because we cannot see Him, cannot tell
whence He cometh and whither He goeth? Because
a thing is mysterious, it is not therefore magical.
The power of God, and the pervading reach of it,
does not surprise me; but if surprise should begin,
it would not begin at the thought that God was
working in my mind and spirit, the part of me
that proclaims itself to be the highest and the
nearest to God, who is also a Spirit. None that
believes in God but knows that all his members
are knit together by God's power, and will dissolve
to dust when that is withdrawn. If God takes
order for the contracting muscle, and the throbbing
pulse, and the vibrations of the ear, there is nothing wild or incredible in the thought that the
*S*pirit of God condescends to His degraded name-
sake, the spirit of man, and there takes order by
laws of His own for its life and government.

Let it be tried, not as dreams and fancies are tried, but as you judge the historical facts of the gospel. The waves of Galilee swayed the boat of Jesus close to the shore, on which eager listeners crowded to hear Him to the very edge. We know it was so, because those that knew have set it down for us. If we would assail the fact, we must assail the witness. And are there, then, no witnesses that the Spirit has dwelt where He was promised to dwell, in the believing souls, ever since Christ departed ? All the rich centuries of Christian history answer that there are. Poor as they are for a thousand losses and disappointments, they yet can bring us proof of life, and of the same life which, unless they are the very footprints of the present Spirit, are unaccountable to us. Of the same life. Who does not admit the brotherhood of them that have lived for the gospel and suffered for the gospel · in all lands and times? The Stephens and Polycarps who bled for Christ long since are own brothers to the Mackenzies, who, for want of a little healing powder, droop and die as but yesterday for Christ. The difference between them is that between the mellow distance and the hard and vulgar foreground. Paul, weighed down with the care of all the Churches he had founded, is felt to be a brother, in many a trait of character, in many a word of true comfort, by the clergyman who, this very day, in some new parish in the repulsive outskirts of some uninviting town, is trying to kindle the spiritual life, and keep it alive when kindled, without which man's life is but a kind of death, a death with dreams. By sure witness to plain facts are we able to believe that what Christ promised has come to pass. As Christ went so the Spirit came. Both are.facts, and to be proved and examined as facts. But we are told it was expedient for the disciples that Christ should depart. It was good for them that their Master should be taken from their head ; and He who tells them so is the Master Himself. It *was* expedient. After He had left them they did become braver, stronger, more independent and outspoken. The presence of a friend whom they tenderly loved and wished to obey was not so favourable to their growth as the presence within them of the Spirit, helping their infirmities, suggesting thoughts higher than they knew, and giving to their purposes a novel strength. It was better that, instead of counsel, they should know freedom of the will ; that instead of leaning on the sufficient strength of a mighty friend, they should feel an imparted strength.

Let us lay these startling words of Christ to heart.
There are not wanting signs of a desire to rest
upon the corporeal presence of Christ, or some
substitute for it, rather than on the felt indwelling
of the Spirit of God. Amongst Christians, statues
that came from a heathen sculptor's chisel are
named anew, and men kneel and worship them,
hoping thereby to get nearer to God. He was
nearer to them than they thought. He was within
them, taking hold with them of the burden of their
infirmities if they would have suffered Him. With
this intimate nearness, the wood or stone does nothing to bring Him nearer. Nay, coming nearer
home, may we not do well to remember, when we
yearn for Christ's presence, that He will be present
only as He has promised? He is not here, locally
present, to be regarded with adoring eyes, and yet
He is here, to be by us received in a spiritual
manner, and by the Spirit's help we may feed on
Him in our hearts by faith with thanksgiving.

Let me conclude. " Know ye not that ye are
the temple of God, and that the Spirit of God
dwelleth in you? If any man defile the temple of
God, him shall God destroy: for the temple of God
is holy, which temple ye are," (1 Cor. iii. 16, 17.)
Awful words! They plead against impurity and

dissoluteness with a great power. They are answered by the echoes of many a ruined temple,
"Him shall God destroy." Of the great ruin
hereafter I need not now speak; but let us think
of the *present* ruin. A young mind is set apart
by God to be His temple, and the Spirit of God
shall be the fire upon the altar, and prayers,
prompted by the Spirit, shall be its incense; and
worldly thoughts and longings shall be brought
before the altar, to be sacrificed as its reasonable
service. Round about it there are natural fences
to keep out the unclean beasts that might defile it.
Filial deference, natural modesty and shame, the
thought that we must not lavish what has been
stored for us by loving thrift; these are not godli-
ness, but they are natural fences against some
temptations. A good religious training, our prayers
in the past, and good resolutions; these are the
stones out of which such a temple is built. All
this goodly building is wasted. The limbs sacred
to God are made the members of a harlot; and the
natural shame is stamped out with repeated outrages; and the clear eye and calm speech of reason
are changed into the leer and chatter of a poor
drunkard; and in such indulgence is wasted the
future provision of a mother and sisters, who, pray-

ing at evening in the temperate and pure home far off, do not forget to bless the absent, praying not for his conversion out of a ruin half-accomplished, but only for his continuance in the paths he was taught to walk in. Men speak of the sins of youth with indulgence; and harsh condemnation is not wise—is not true. But let us pity it, this great destiny so foully marred; this peace, and growth, and freedom of will, and calm heart-worship, changed into lust and drunken foolishness, and a broken will, and an eye that looks this way and that lest it should see God. We talk of the severity of God in judging of sin. Consider this rather as a question of the operation of laws. Though there should be no thought but that of mercy, mercy may become impossible. The body that needs daily to be lashed into life by new sinful excitements, the brain perplexed with wine and wantonness, the mind that can find no contentment in its own condition; what could you say of these but that here there is no place for the interceding Spirit, where every hedge is broken and the house ruined. There are no prayers that He, in His loving humiliation, may add His groanings that cannot be uttered; there is no feeling of infirmities as before God, that He might put a hand upon the burden to help to bear it. When the apostle says of them that give themselves to the works of the flesh, " They which do such things shall not inherit the kingdom of God," (Gal. v. 21,) this is not a judgment, but a statement of fact. Oh! my brethren, grieve not the Holy Spirit. Think of every act of shame and riot as tending to silence, and to expel at last, that divine guide from your heart. You remember the legend, that in the doomed city, on the eve of its destruction, voices were heard as of angels deliberating together, and resolving to depart, since they could no more protect. If you should fall into any sin, listen in the stillness of the night for such a voice of threatening within you. Listen, and pray against such a punishment, such a ruin. You shall not pray in vain. Kept safe whilst evils are around you, you shall find your prayers have this mark of their divine origin, that they are in advance of your own experience. You shall pray heartily for grace before you have tasted the savour of grace; you shall ask God for power to follow duty even whilst you feel that the path of duty is not the path of joy. You shall ask that sins may be burned out of you, though they are still too sweet. In this the intercessions of the

Spirit are unutterable, inexplicable ; for they lead us that know not what we ask to ask for higher things than we know. Trust the Spirit to lead you, for He is divine. He is able to guide you into all truth and goodness. He is yours.

XIII.

SHE IS A SINNER.

PREACHED FOR THE ST JAMES'S HOME, LONDON, AN INSTITUTION FOR FALLEN WOMEN OF THE MORE EDUCATED CLASS.

"Now when the Pharisee which had bidden him saw it, he spake within himself, saying, This man, if he were a prophet, would have known who and what manner of woman this is that toucheth him : for she is a sinner."

"SHE is a sinner!" This is the Pharisee's compendious trial and verdict and sentence of one in whose soul, it seems, the sore but wholesome struggle of repentance was actively going on. "She is a sinner;" accursed from God she is and must continue. There is abomination in her touch, and falsehood in her tears. All that a prophet can do for her is to pass her by on the other side. Let her not come here, to shame by her presence those who know her infamy; let the lost herd with the lost; and the dead bury their dead; and let us, the saved and living, be free from their intrusion. Thus reasoned a sincere respectable man among the Jews; not a monster of intolerance, not a brutal scorner of the suffering; but a respectable Jew of the most exact sect among the Jews, speaking in the interests of

Q

society, and echoing an acknowledged social principle. And thus reason many sincere and worthy
men amongst ourselves, almost two thousand years
after the Lord has taught lessons of another spirit
and a more loving wisdom.

Social rules are general, not universal ; and our
danger lies in building on them more than they
will bear. I suppose that experience has taught
most of us that it is as difficult to retrace the steps
along the broad way of sin as it is easy to enter it.
It is no very common thing for the confirmed
drunkard to conquer his depraved yearning ; nor
for the dishonest man to become trustworthy ; nor
for the violent and brutal to learn gentleness. It
is no common thing for a woman like her who
came to wash the Lord's feet, when she has turned
all God's gifts to the uses of folly, and scattered
all her mind and spirit in vanity, and learnt to dis-
guise under gay speech and a defiant manner the
anguish of an inextinguishable shame, to sit down
sober and in her right mind, and repair the rags of
self-respect that still cling to her, and alter the tone
of profane defiance for the tears and exclamations
of the contrite. And society for its own protection
makes a rule, somewhat rough and inexact, that all
who have lost their *character* shall stand under a

social ban, which shall not be removed at all, or at least not without the most patent proofs of recovery. Loss of character, so to speak, is the leprosy of morals; and the unclean shall not mix with the clean; they shall bear the marks of their ailment upon them; and the conditions of cure and re-instatement are so remote as almost to preclude hope.

Nor must we expect that this will ever be completely changed. Men see not with the eye of God; the heart is hid from them, they can but judge the acts. The most determined murderer may plan and secretly execute his destroying work in the midst of us, and it is not until some miscalculation of his, or some unusual vigilance of others, unmasks him, that the social circle recoils from around him in horror. What can we do, then, but watch the actions, and rate men by the only standard, to speak generally, to which we have access? But our measure is very inexact, the sentences we pronounce often wrong. How different is the judgment of Him who came to seek and save the lost! What would have become of the whole human race, if the broken and contrite heart had been despised by Him, because it had once beaten with the pulses of a guilty excitement? if He had been as ready as we are to break the bruised reed of a weak will, and quench the smoking flax of an incipient penitence? For just observe how the harsh judgments of society tend to increase the sin which they condemn. No one at first throws himself or herself headlong into guilt, sinning with all the heart and soul, without casting one look backward upon the state of comparative peace he is leaving. The descent into the gulf of lost souls is a stair and not a precipice, and upon the first steps the feet falter, and the hands grope vaguely to meet the firm grasp of a friend, if haply one will arrest them before they disappear from the face of day. If the sinner, at the moment when return is possible, sees behind him only faces of scorn, and hears only the hum of many voices crying out shame, he prefers too often the sympathy of vice to the austere rebuke of self-satisfied virtue, and hastens on to the level of those who are worse than himself; where, at least, there are none to point the finger of scorn at him. And yet how various are the grades of offence which the world includes in one sweeping condemnation! "She is a sinner," says the Pharisee in the text. One word suffices to classify all that have gone astray; he makes no inquiries, draws no distinctions, indulges no hopes. It is all one to him whether a depraved will or a giddy vanity made her a willing victim, or the sheer pressure of starvation drove her to ruin. It is all one whether, every day when she rises, and every night when she lies down, she hates herself, and in bitter anguish compares the thing she is with what she was; or acquiesces in her own destruction, and does all she can to hasten the darkness that is settling down upon her moral nature, and to welcome the perfect night. It is this fatal precipitation in judging; it is this loose and general estimate that we are too lazy to correct; it is this want of hearty faith in the Healer of Spirits which makes us stand with our hands hanging down in the midst of an appalling amount of sin, some of which, at least, if we would only copy our Redeemer, and deal with our erring fellow-creatures in the spirit of mercy in which He deals with us, we should be able to remove. We pass our hasty sentence upon thousands and tens of thousands of erring beings, not considering for a moment how many among them are devoured by an unspeakable remorse; how many are capable of sorrow, though they stave it off; how few comparatively are the hopeless children of perdition, lost in this world and the world to come.

Now there are two facts which may well make us pause ere we adopt the hard and thoughtless rule of society in dealing with guilt; and they *are* facts, and not mere surmises. The one is incontestably proved by the careful inquiries of sensible and benevolent men. It is, that society is in a large measure responsible for the very sins which it so readily condemns and casts out. If we could deduct from that astounding total of guilt, which so shocks the moralist and utterly perplexes the statesman, all that has been brought about by the pressure of positive want, and by treachery and deceived hopes; if, in a word, we could strike off all that has been caused by the very classes which are so prompt with their condemnation, the sum of what remained would be small indeed by comparison. It may be said that society is not answerable for the poverty which is the most frequent cause of sin. I will not dispute this wide question; but whether we have taken every pains to teach poor people to guard against thoughtless habits; whether we have seen that the labour we employ is fairly remunerated, so that none who work for us shall have the dread alternative offered them of sinning or starving; whether the lawful claims of the poor to a maintenance are always fairly met—

are questions upon which, to say the least, two opinions might be held. But all that I now argue for is, that if the operation of social rules has in any measure caused sin, we that make and uphold social rules should deal considerately with the sinner. Even if it be an imperfection, and not an inherent wickedness in our social arrangements, that causes them to generate sin, we must not be too ready to visit on the erring, guilt which is only their own in part, guilt which they groan under, and perhaps would fain be delivered from. Imagine a friendless woman in this great city, working from the dawn of one day till the strokes of midnight announced the next, to earn at the week's end a sum that might almost be told in pence; think of the time when, after bearing up long against hunger and weakness, hope gave way, and the fruitless industry was abandoned; think of the misery endured by a mind tutored for better things in eating the bread of sin, whilst it was known that the wages of sin is death. Follow her as she rushes forth some inclement night, clutching to her side her child, the one humanising influence left to her by a merciful God, determined to turn from sin, and hide herself from besetting temptations in no better sanctuary than a workhouse. See her sink

down in the snow at a door, her child's feet frozen
to her side, and she fainting from starvation. And
when the good Samaritan that lives there has
opened the door, and set food before her, and
rubbed back the life into the numbed limbs,
she shall go on her way and seek entrance at the
workhouse door, which would be to her as the
outer porch of the gates of heaven, for sin would
be shut out behind her; and she shall be rejected,
no doubt by rule, for some formality which has not
been complied with; and she shall fall back again
into the old life of guilt, shame, and sorrow. And
the well-dressed passer-by, wearing on his back the
labour of her fingers, paid for at the rate of three-
pence for nineteen continuous hours, avoids her
path, and whispers, " She is a sinner." *Did* I say
imagine? It is a true tale, to which not even one
particular has been added. She, indeed, escaped
at last, for great is the mercy and love of God; but
others have suffered and not escaped. And when
we are told that not in one case, but in hundreds,
this tragedy is being acted over and over again—
the incident different, the catastrophe the same—
we must, if we are honest, change the Pharisaic
formula. " She is a sinner," for one that is more
humane—" She is a great sufferer, sick in soul

may the Lord take her to the arms of His mercy!"

Now, let us give due weight to the other fact—that there is hardly any escape for those who have once entered the path of sin. Where should a woman like this one of my text betake herself for a shelter, when she tastes the bitterness of her degradation, and longs eagerly to escape from it? The door of her home is often shut against her; the home affections that once refreshed her flow no longer towards her. Unblemished character is an indispensable condition for almost any safe employment; and the most sincere and heartfelt repentance would not stand instead of it. We seem to bid her fill up the measure of her sin; we will not help her to escape. "*She is a sinner;*" no one will take her into a blameless home to employ her; no one will visit her and give her counsel. The consciousness that she belongs now to a class of outcasts fills her with shame; and the more that feeling exists, the less likely is she to return into the presence of those who might be able to restore her. Thus does one step in sin utterly destroy one whom God created to serve and praise Him. God bids the sinner turn from evil ways; and we will give her no chance of turning. Christ came to turn every one of us from his iniquities; and we interpose against one form of sin. He was sent to bind up the broken-hearted, to proclaim liberty to the captives, and the opening of the prison to them that are bound; and who are we that we should neglect a breaking heart and its agonising cry, and leave captives groaning in a bondage of sin worse than death? There is not perhaps one point upon which the world of professing Christians has more strongly resisted the gospel than this. We tend the sick because our Lord has bidden us; and there is not one large town without its hospital. We teach the poor; we build churches for worship; we set up clubs and charitable institutions for physical wants. But very few have been the Houses of Refuge in which a penitent woman may hide her shame, and find, instead of scorn, some portion of that spirit in which our Saviour said of one like her, that came and shed the tears of repentance upon His feet, and wiped them with the hair she had once been vain of, " Her sins, which are many, are forgiven, for she loved much : but to whom little is forgiven, the same loveth little."

Within the last few years earnest efforts have been made to grapple with this great difficulty, and to efface this black stain upon a Christian

nation ; and the Institution for. which your aid is
asked to-day has this to interest us, that it marks
the second epoch in the history of penitentiaries
for fallen women. It is the first attempt in this
country to *classify* the cases of moral disease. The
prisoners in a well-ordered jail are all parted into
classes; in every workhouse, in every hospital for
the sick, the same principle is applied. In all these
cases the principle of classification was adopted
late, after the attempt to do without had been
found, after experience, to fail. You might see
even now in a foreign prison, as I have done, the
professional thief and the student whose only crime
has been a copy of verses or a declamation on
liberty, shut up for months together in the narrow
precincts of a single room; but no one can well
doubt that the student will come out a worse
citizen for that so-called correction ; every hour
and minute of which has been a moral torture to
him, such as no power has the right to inflict on
any man. The attempt to classify, to separate
dissimilar cases, and provide appropriate treatment
for each, is a sign that the work has made progress,
and that experience has been gained in dealing
with it. This "Home for Penitents" has been
opened for two classes of the fallen ; for those who

have descended from a somewhat higher station in
society, and for those whose career of sin and
shame has not been so long as to harden them to
the utmost. It is not at all intended to establish
in the former class what may be called an aristo-
cracy of guilt; nor to countenance the notion that
sin which has retained some small vestige of refine-
ment, is on that account less heinous, less deplorable. The Committee, in an excellent Report, tell
us that "their experience leads them to fear that
the higher the birth and education, the more depraved must be the nature to occasion a wilful
wandering away from the path of virtue, where
temptations to wickedness are so few." It is not
because they are better, then, but because their
treatment is more difficult, that they are to be set
apart. Many of them are quite unfit for hard
work; they have lost all that is best in a woman,
but retain a woman's repugnance to coarse manners
and speech. If they were placed in an ordinary
refuge, to spend their time in hard manual labour
in the company of those who have received no
education and are further brutalised by vice, their
resolution to amend, never very strong, would give
way sooner or later. In a work so difficult as the
restoration of a sinner, let us remove every obstacle

that will give way to human hands : if this separate
treatment will save one sister the more, let it be
fairly tried. But up to this time the experiment
has not been made completely. Besides the Home
itself, a little way removed, it is very desirable to
open one or more houses into which, upon the first
impulse of remorse, the sinner may hasten, and find
shelter, and encouragement, and strength. Most of
these unhappy beings are incapable of forming a
fixed purpose of good. The moral nature is utterly
broken down under a course of shameful excess.
An assumed joy, attained too often by the help of
poisonous stimulants, alternates with the deepest depression. The actions are impulsive as a
child's. Whether the lost one shall come in to the
Christian comforter that would bring her back to
the ways of peace, or crown her sins by suicide,
depends upon an impulse, not upon a choice.

Open the door, then, of some house where, at
any hour of day or night, the daughter of sin may
find herself welcome. Let her know where it is ;
let it be near the haunts where the fallen act out
their life of guilt; let them point at it as they
flaunt past with a smile or a sneer ; some of them
will remember it one day when their hearts are too
heavy for sneers, and it may be their harbour of

refuge from a devouring sea. This is what we are
called upon to aid·in by our alms to-day. This is
what is needed to put this excellent institution in
possession of the complete means of good.

Let there be no extravagant expectations of the
results of such an institution. The task it proposes
to itself is hard beyond description. In an hospital
for the body a few days often suffice to work a
cure; the moral diseases are all chronic, and need
a patient treatment. Sometimes the hope that
new habits are forming is suddenly disappointed
by a relapse; but still the course of repentance has
in many cases resulted in a restoration to piety and
a virtuous mode of life. In this Home, just established, the results are small as yet, yet they are
real and definite. If only one had been rescued
from perdition since it has been at work, all the
cost and the devoted labour that have been be-
stowed on it would have been richly repaid.

Now, is there one that can hear of an institution
like this, without giving it his sympathy and his
prayers? We are verily guilty concerning our
sister; there is no escape from that. We have set
traps in her way that she may stumble, and made
it most difficult for her to rise again. And when
once that most excellent workmanship of God is

defaced, hard indeed is it 'to restore the divine
impress, and recover the lost• proportion. The
affections deadened, the temper soured by scorn,
the mind becomes frivolous and fickle as a child's,
the tastes degraded. Such are the details of ruin,
and the process of restoration must be slow, because it must be systematic, and time is required
to show whether any permanent good is really done.
'The desultory exhortation will do little here, and
the occasional kind word. What is required is an
education wholly new. How can this be given
unless the patient, sequestered from all impure
associations, and safe from fear of want, shall be
trained for a year or two in habits of virtue ? It is
plain, then, that without a house for penitents,
private exertion would do little or no good. So
that this is the only mode in which the rescue of
the fallen can be attempted with good hopes of
success. Man, whose own sins have been visited
by no social penalty, though peradventure not less
in guilt than those which have consigned her to
infamy and a grave, do what you can for restitution.
Doubtless there is a God that judgeth the earth.
And if man sins, and woman bears the fearful
punishment, all that we know of the world's government tells us that that at least cannot be

suffered to continue to the end. In the class of
cases with which ⸱this institution is to deal, are
found not so much the victims of poverty as of
man's falsehood and deceit. The woman, perhaps,
was drawn from virtue by professions of a love
which she hoped would be both lawful and perpetual. She lives for a few years in luxury, to be
the toy of his leisure, to whom she has given up
all her heart. By and by the dream ends. The
man marries another, and the woman begins to
descend through all the grades of ruin. The man
is looked up to by an innocent wife, though there
is one dark chamber in his past life into which he
dare not let her peep. Innocent children gladden
his home with their voices. Where is the woman
who listened to his first vows? A drunken maniac,
blaspheming in the midnight streets, with all her
beauty blotted and defaced; in a year or two she
will be forgotten in a pauper's grave. Yet doubtless there is a God that judgeth the earth, who will
not suffer this unequal measure to continue for ever.
That two should sin together, and one should bear
a twofold portion of the punishment that the back
of the other may be safe from the smiter—this
cannot be just, cannot be the plan of God. What
will you do for restitution? Will you make up

again that defaced image to its former beauty and
purity? You could as easily put back last year's
leaves upon the trees again, or curtain the bright
sun with last year's eclipse. But this you can do:
you can help the efforts that are made to snatch
such as she is out of ruin. You can tell other men
that the destruction of women rests in fact with
them, and that to have taken any part in that foul
conspiracy of the strong sex against the weak is
not what will bring a man peace at the last. Be
not so ready to take a desponding view of the condition of the fallen; is not Christ the well of life,
out of which fountains of recreative water flow;
and cannot He who recalled Lazarus to life, and
made the deaf hear and the lame walk, work
wonders of renewal in the breast of the repentant?
Woman, whose earthly happiness lies in the honour
and love of husband, children, friends, do not fail
to recollect that of the outcasts of society who 'lull'
the incommunicable pangs of shame to sleep by
the treacherous anodyne of drink, and who look
with longing, as to a bed of down for the weary,
upon the deep water that rushes under the bridge,
—many a one began life with better promise, perhaps with as fair as yourself. Round her cradle

R

affectionate hopes gathered, and the prayer of a mother sanctified her sleep; and the first lisping words were shaped into prayers. And as she grew, her very presence was a household blessing; the old man sitting at the hearth would part with all that he possessed to save her from the contact of dishonour. All is gone now; the day that opened so fairly is now the blackness of darkness. Nothing remains but to take the lost sister by the hand, and speak to her the strange words of comfort; to awaken her to the godly sorrow which worketh repentance unto salvation, and so issueth in true peace. Our benign Lord has taught us that even the lost may be gathered back; that even when men, too indolent to inquire and discriminate, pronounce the ruin final, the divine Spirit can rekindle the scattered sparks of love, and warm the cold heart. Let the magistrate or the legislator, who knows well that our political institutions consult for the happiness of each citizen, and are so far imperfect as they fail to do so, remember how unequally they deal with this class; how careful they are of human life there, how prodigal here. We have often seen able judges and consummate advocates occupied for days in the trial of one criminal; and we may be proud that, although the voice of the people may have already pronounced for his guilt, prejudice has been laid aside, and the guilty wretch has received the same dispassionate hearing as if his case was absolutely new. So careful are we lest through prejudice the life of an innocent man should fall! And yet, such is our impotence, that where we see thousands of poor creatures treading the path of certain destruction, we can devise no law to prevent or even palliate the social grievance. The task has been found too difficult by every legislature. But not to offer facilities for the return of those who have found how bitter is the fruit of that whereof the conscience is ashamed, would be a criminal supineness. But, God be thanked for it! what the law could not do, the private exertions of the good are beginning to bring about. The pure and refined devote themselves to the care of the lost; they bear with many cases of disappointment; they suffer wayward tempers, and are content with the slow dawnings of good. And they ask for the help of all Christian people, for the prayers of all who love the Lord Jesus Christ in sincerity. If we have known any consolation in Christ, let us aid in

bringing the lost sheep back to their true Shepherd; that instead of the torments of remorse, and
the fear of a dreadful future, they may hear the
word pronounced by Christ, "Her sins, which are
many, are forgiven."

XIV.

HONOUR ALL MEN.

PREACHED IN WESTMINSTER ABBEY, 1866

"Honour all men. Love the brotherhood. Fear God. Honour
the king."

O F this well-known text, which has been read
in the Epistle for this day, I want but one
part out of four to occupy us this evening. "Honour all men." Christ our Lord, who first showed
humanity its degradation by convincing it of sin,
has taught the world what no other teacher ever
took up, the worth and dignity of men.

"Honour all men. . . . Honour the king." It is
the same word in both cases. The apostle is not
careful to abate the honour due to men by some
weaker expression. Honour is the thing due to
king and to man. But in the Greek the tense is different; honour all men as various occasions arise for
it; but in the other three cases, the object and the
occasion are known; give present love and fear
and honour to a visible brotherhood, and a present
God and a known ruler. It is as though the apostle

prefaced the special precepts with this more general one. Honour all men everywhere; nothing is to annul this, the charter of the whole redeemed race; but specially love the Christian brotherhood, and fear the God so visibly present among them, and honour the appointed king.

All are lost; all are precious. These are the two ground-tones of Christianity. All are lost but for Christ; all are precious in the sight of Christ. Never before the time of the apostles had the baseness of humanity been so manifest. In the despised Galilean corner of Jewry, despised by the world, had a jewel of price been found, that had ennobled and enriched those that found it; but they trampled it under swinish feet, and turned again to rend the hand that sent it. Christ was that jewel. Was there no eye to see its preciousness? no touchstone left amongst a corrupted people to discern the pure metal of His golden truth? Sin looked on that which was most holy, and knew not that it was holy, and hated it for its strangeness. Jewish hands slew the King of the Jews, the Lord of glory. They filled up the cup of their guilt to overflowing. What more was needed to make them accursed from God? But the preachers that showed them their sin lifted them up with that other truth. "See what love hath God shown to the world! When we were yet sinners Christ died for us ungodly; died that we might live." Precious must those be for whom He came to die. Great must be the destiny, rich the birthright, would they but claim it, of those on whose behalf Christ transacted for restoration. And these two sides of the gospel have ever gone together. Until the gospel has come, whether to a nation or to the conscience of a man, the deep taint and degradation of sin has never been understood; but the same gospel has taught reverence for these beings so degraded, so corrupt. They were lost; but they have been saved. They have served the devil; but God made them a little lower than the angels. Sin has sealed them with the stamp of death; but the fire of an immortal hope burns in their heart. "What God has cleansed, that call not thou common," (Acts x. 15.)

And so the spirit that resists the gospel may be expected always to strike at both these truths. Where moral corruption prevails, sin is made light of, on one hand, and men, their motives, their rights, their self-respect, are outraged, on the other. Where philosophical conceit resists the truth, the line that severs sin from goodness is carefully erased on one side; and on the other the position and hopes of men are brought down to the level of those of the beasts that perish.

1. Man is honourable among the creatures of God for his *knowledge* and power of thought. Other natures feel and suffer and enjoy their portion in the great scheme of nature; man lifts himself and looks around, and attempts to understand the whole of the scheme. The harmonies and beauties which God, who made them, saw to be good when they were made, we too can admire. Once this wonderful universe existed but as a thought in the mind of the Most High, until He willed that it should start forth full of power, and life, and beauty, and enjoyment. You close your eyes; and for you too—I speak it reverently—the universe exists as thought. Not merely are the gorgeous frag-ments of that great picture imprinted in the memory; and the night of stars, and the fresh sea, and the strange forms of vegetation in the tropical jungle, and the enormous forces of waterfall, and earthquake, and volcano, capable of being recalled, but the mind can see somewhat of their form and order, of their succession in time, of their natural action and reaction, of the laws that govern them. And so whilst other creatures swim, as it were, sub-

merged in the great ocean of being, man, and he alone, lifts himself above it, and sees afar off the great sun, that gives it light and life. Other creatures are of the world; man is at once within it and above it, a partaker and a spectator of this wonderful creation. Far above us, the great Lord looks upon this world, the emanation from His thought and will, and pronounces it to be good; and here below our weak voice, heard of Him above the roar of all winds and waters and the hum of a myriad forms of life, answers "Yes; we too can see that it is good." This great universe, which comes to other creatures as a minister of food and drink, of rest, of energy, of satisfaction, and fatigue, is clothed upon by man with ideas which enlighten him alone, and the cold outlines of material facts are tinged with the colours of beauty, and symmetry, and wisdom, and bounty. By the light of God that is in him, man sees God in the world of matter and life. The finger print of the most wise artificer is upon every part. Only one creature is able to say, "Lo! His hand has been here."

2. But that which is at once the glory and the shame of man, is his power to choose, his will. Man is in some sense free. More than a passive spectator of nature, he takès advantage of his

knowledge. With natural laws in his hand for his instruments, he puts nature under his feet. The road which nature has made for him in one place, he imitates and surpasses in places where there was none. He uproots the plant from one soil and forces it to grow in another, nearer to his needs; nay, when it droops and languishes, he cheers it with artificial moisture and shelter, so as to transplant the climate with the root. The same great Creator who gave him the eye to see it, has given him the power and the will to have dominion over it. He is the visible king of nature, the viceroy of the great King that made it. How has he fulfilled his trust? Let the long history of wars and robberies bear witness to his ferocity; let the large tracts of barbarism and ignorance that reach over half the world bear witness to his supineness.

3. And this power of action is also a power of obedience to the law of God. Oh that ennobling and yet reproving voice of conscience, which, once that it is heard, proves that we are citizens of a heavenly city! Oh that voice within, which nothing human has suggested, which says, "Thou hast sinned against the Lord!" What can it mean, even though thou silence it, less than this, that thou art a straying servant from another

realm, whose Lord has sent a messenger clothed with authority to bring thee home again? Once we have heard it, we know that we are not all of this world. Higher wants, higher laws, there must be, than those we can find among material things or in the animal part of us. Drown it you may with roistering and dissipation; you may outrage it with crimes; you may cover it over deep enough with the hard level pavement of a plodding, sensual selfishness. Yet it will one day wake again. "After all, thou hast sinned." No one knows when it will find you; may it only be soon! It may come when mind and body, weary with sin, lie open to its timely rebuke. It may come when life is almost over, and can only water its past with tears. It may come when life is over, from the lips of the judge. Come when it will, it comes from God, and we cannot gainsay it.

4. And, lastly, man is immortal. "God is not the God of the dead, but of the living," (Matt. xxii. 32.) I know that this truth is one not gathered from reason alone. Man's knowledge, and will, and conscience, no one can choose but see. But upon man's immortality Christianity alone has spoken clearly out. Reason and science have never abandoned the hope; but they have uttered

it with stammering lips. We are immortal, for Christ has awakened us to hopes which are too large and too high for this life. We are immortal, for the hope of a future life, awakened and fostered by our Lord, cannot be meant to end in a delusion. We are immortal, for holiness is possible for us, a new nature can be formed in us, a nature that is God's own work, and is accompanied by a thirst for the presence of God. We are immortal, because, without that, all that is best and purest in us would lead us to deceit and delusion. Those who live out this life as the vestibule to another wherein they shall see God, can these indeed be deceived? Can they have staked their life upon promises that shall not be kept? Was Stephen's vision of glory, whereby he was able to triumph in the supreme agony of death, no real revelation? Was Paul's crown of righteousness a mere dream, and his desire to be with Christ to end in mere annihilation? No; the soul, once clothed on with holiness, knows that this radiant marriage-garment is a passport to the presence of the King that makes the feast. They doubt about immortality, to whom the thought brings more fear than clear hope. "He that doeth the will of God abideth for ever," (1 John ii. 17.) This is the assurance of those

that seek Him. To have known the way of the
Lord here is to be sure that we have received "a
kingdom that cannot be moved," (Heb. xii. 28.)

Honour all men; honour those to whom God
has given the discerning soul, and the deciding
will, and the guiding conscience, and the inheritance of eternal life.

Here we are met at all points by those who
question every one of these attributes, and strive
to persuade man to abandon all his rights in God
and in a future world.

Every faculty that you have, and every organ,
you possess in common with lower animals. Your
eminence is only one of degree. Between the
brain of the higher ape and your own it would
perplex you to establish any generic difference.
To reason is not your prerogative, but only to
reason somewhat better than the beasts. Nay,
your separation from the beasts is but a question
of time. Favourable circumstances of climate and
nourishment have lifted up the best ape into the
lowest man; and this is our parentage. Hopes
for the future must all be of the same kind. Given
a few millions of years, during which the present
race of men shall grow, and fall, and rot, like crops
of leaves, and the better specimens of our race, by

a kind of upward yearning, shall found a higher race still. Thus, and thus only, are hopes of a higher existence to be satisfied ; whatever goes beyond this is egotism and delusion.

It is remarkable that there is no evidence of any such transition from one species to another ; if such changes had taken place, the earth, so rich in fossil records of past forms of life, would have preserved us examples of the periods of transition. But on that I will not insist. If it be true indeed that there is no fundamental difference between the organs of the thinking word-dividing man, and the jibbering ape, whilst yet the fruits by which we know them are so different, then, I think, we must seek for the causes of their difference elsewhere than in the organs. Materialism has striven after too much. If she has succeeded in finding all the parts of man's brain, presented also in the ape, then we may breathe a little after all these imperious demands of science. Newton's powers of combination, and Shakespeare's mind peopled with a little world of thinking men and women, and Raphael's forms and Handel's harmonies, we may now admire them for themselves ; we are no longer obliged to view them as so much brain, there is not difference enough in the organs to account for a difference of result that is in fact immeasurable. The Bible recognises all through that man is woven together of spirit and matter, of thoughts, feelings, emotions, in which the body bears a large part. In our temptations, in the emotions of love and gratitude, whereby we rise above those temptations, the flesh, the body, now opposes, now ministers to the soul. We do not disown our kindred with the dust. Our complex bodily system is, in some sense, an epitome of all lower organisms. But the more you bring us down to the level of the beasts, the more do you abandon all attempts to give any material explanation of the greatness of man. By divine ordinance, man does understand the world, does govern the world, keeps the keys of the garden of thought, so full of wonder and of beauty. The lower creatures quail before that front sublime ; they flee, or else they bow their docile neck under the yoke that man lays on them. Be it that science still suspects the brain is apish : then the world's permitted master has done wonders with that inadequate brain.

Nor are we allowed to cling to those thoughts of conscience, duty, and immortality which seem to us so plainly sent from God, which seem bright still with the light of the heaven from whence they

S

came. Thought, they tell us, is a material product, a secretion of the brain; how, then, can it have any power, any witness to bear, beyond the world wherein it originated, or any destiny more permanent than that of the short-lived, decaying organ from which it sprung? All the thoughts which seem to have a higher scope should be adjusted to some present use and need; otherwise they are mere delusion.

This attempt to liken thought to other functions of the body is so great a fallacy that I wonder it has been seriously made. All bodily functions subserve the main purpose of the whole organism. They preserve its life, by renewing what is wasted, and by removing all that is effete and decayed. The instincts for seeking food, and for self-defence, and defence of progeny, are in the same way subservient to the general purpose of the living body, and tend to keep up the life which God has given it. But thought, in the true sense of that word, does not subserve, it dominates the body. We want a new definition of the word "organ," if it is to apply to that which uses the whole living creature as its instrument, carries it whither it would. not, wears it out, destroys it, casts it aside. History will show you, for example, a whole nation.

infected with a passion for warlike glory. For that idea it poured out its blood like water; every strong man went forth to die, went willingly, at the bidding of a selfish ruler, and left boys and broken old men alone to reap the yellow corn and gather the purple grape. Hundreds of thousands died for that idea ; and a whole nation lay panting with exhaustion. And yet this thought, forsooth, was only a function of each man's brain. This is not the behaviour of an organ of our system. As well call the stormy wind that swallowed up a brave ship in the Channel a function or a product of the masts that bent before its fury. Or, take another example. I see a band of poor men, poor in purse, in repute, in education, and the thought has taken possession of them, that by preaching the story of a Friend who was crucified, and who rose out of His grave, they will shed a new light abroad upon the world, and work a moral reformation by means of a new hope of immortality through holiness. Friends, I daresay, advised them to get rid of that delusion. It was no delusion : it became true. It carried them whither they would not ; and, so far as we know, almost all of them were slain for this their thought. But the Church of Christ on earth is the fruit of their work,

and all men and women built up in holy ways and
wishes are their work ; and this church, in which
we are gathered to-night, is the same thought expressed in stone, and all our worship here to-night
had never been but for their steadfast adhesion to
their thought. It is a mere confusion of words to
speak of thought as a function of any organ of the
body ; were it so, it would subserve the body, and
the body would resist and restrain all in which it
went beyond the due subjection of an organ to the
purpose of the whole system. Because it is too
great for that, I must conceive thought as set in
motion by something outside the body, of which
the whole man is the organ. That something is
the power of the Maker. There, and at no lower
height, you find a cause sufficient for that effect.
If it is at the touch of God that the highest of His
creatures is quickened into thought, then there is
no more wonder that the thoughts are larger than
the world could have suggested, that they rule the
body instead of being controlled by it, that they
give us the first hints of a heaven which we have
not seen, of a life of self-denying duty which the
lazy body would have had no part in inventing.
But you insist that the brain has still a share in it ?
Be it so. He that made the body can use it. Be-

cause thought is implicated with the brain, it is not therefore the brain. I stood once among mountains to see the first dawn of a bright day. The sun, not yet visible to me, sent across the heaven the first sign of his presence, a rose-flush on a snowy peak. Had the sun been fixed there for ever, who would have been certain that the rosy hue was not part of the mountain itself? How would you have proved to a child, without elaborate arguments, that that rosy tint passed invisible over its head, and only came into visible existence upon the pale snow and dull crags, thousands and thousands of miles from the source of light? We are such children when the light of mind and spirit are in question. And when St Paul, sitting in a prison from which he may well think he shall not escape, sees all things round him, even the coldness of friends and the rough world, lighted with the flush of heaven, we cannot see the light as it passes out of heaven into a prisoner's cell. But he is "the prisoner of the Lord," and the Lord is with him; and the thoughts that pass through his mind, and cheer that worn frame, weary of its earthly life, are thoughts from the God of all light.

Yes; honour all men. They are polluted with

sin ; most of them are content in their pollution.
Yet honour and treasure that ruined image of God
which He has made to think, which He has en-
abled to choose and to will ; honour those for whom
· Jesus died, whose conscience is still a witness for
God, a witness that, if it sleeps, may be awakened,
whose heritage is immortality, who may be fashioned again into His likeness.

And is there no practical result from such
speculations ? In a great city like this, the greatest of its many miseries is, that to suit the wants
of the stronger many of the weaker are used as
mere means and implements. Go, man of science,
if you wish for proofs against us, to those whom
our civilisation has ground and crushed, go to those
artisans, skilled and industrious, but whom religious teaching has not reached ; many of them are
already prepared to admit that they look for no
higher life, nor higher ruler, than what is daily
visible to them. Half-seen under the lamplight,
the ruined creatures, whom a sensual capital has
used and cast away, as though God did not make
them, glide about our streets and shame us. The
workman that clothes us, or that fashions the pretty
jewel that is to glisten on a round arm at a queen's
court, you turned him from his two rooms because

you wanted a nobler building ; he found one room afar off, and then, stifled and depressed, he fell sick, and he is in a workhouse sick-room, and his babes are in a workhouse nursery, where well-meaning people will honestly try to give him such tending as is consistent with careful repression of the rates. He is in danger of passing from one of those to whom we owe honour, for Christ's sake, into a thing, into one of the broken potsherds of our great feast, broken by accident and swept off carefully, that the feast may still go well and seemly. Then, it is a fact that in this capital, full of meat and luxury, men do starve to death. One reads that they die of some ailment "aggravated by exposure and want of food." That is the technical phrase. We may say God made them to live their time out ; men let them die. Oh, these things are worth your thoughts. It is more profitable far to brood over them in silence than to indulge in tumid talk about improvements and the general prosperity. To cast the blame on this law or that administrator, may be no part of our duty. But every Christian man and woman is bound, I think, to do a little for those who, honoured by a *Saviour's* love as much as we, are in danger of sinking into mere tools of those who are stronger than they

What can we do? What? is there no place that
wants the light of comfort, and looks to you to ad-
minister it? Then you are poor indeed. But there
is no one of whom this can truly be said. Look
round for those whom you are to comfort, and go
forth to comfort them. You will find your best
confirmation of your faith in the gospel by doing
the works of the gospel. To treat other men, trod-
den down in misery and ignorance, as immortal
beings dear to Christ, will deepen your own faith in
immortality, and your own sense of the presence
of Christ. " Inasmuch as ye have done it unto one
of the least of these my brethren, ye have done it
unto me," (Matt. xxv. 40.)

XV.

SOCIAL SCIENCE.

*PREACHED IN YORK MINSTER BEFORE THE SOCIAL
SCIENCE CONGRESS,* 1865.

"Man goeth forth unto his work, and to his labour, until the evening. O Lord, how manifold are thy works! in wisdom hast
thou made them all : the earth is full of thy riches."

IN this marvellous psalm the works of God are
called up one after another, as it were to
praise God, until the whole creation, sea and land,
sky and earth, beast and fish, seem to join in one
swelling hymn of praise, and to glow with the
light and to be quickened with the life of God
that is in them. Man's share in this great psalm
is somewhat brief, and yet most significant. Two
short sentences are almost all. "Man goeth forth
to his work, and to his labour, until the evening."
. . . "Let the sinners be consumed out of the
earth, and let the wicked be no more," (ver. 23, 35.)
Man, like the rest of creation, goes about his work
from sunrise to sunset, guided by the same wisdom that laid the foundations of the earth, gave

the lion its instinct, and appointed the sun and moon their function. The Bible does not reveal what man was to discover for himself for his own education; and it does not therefore disclose social laws, or display the perfect pattern of a political system, or set its stamp upon a particular method of education. But it tells us that all God's works are made " in His wisdom," and are guided by His power. If science, as her last effort, shall proceed to group her historical materials, and discover in social facts a method and an order analogous to what she found amongst the starry spheres, amongst the many elements of this solid earth, amongst the brutes that in their small circle of life obey that God who is their light with an invariable submission, there is nothing in this discovery which, at the outset, ought to startle us. Order is the watchword of the universe; how, then, could man fail to learn it? Law is the expression of God's will; how, then, could man escape from its operation? Man comes from God, His last, His greatest work; marred and defaced indeed, yet still His work. The marks of that divine Artificer are upon him still. "O Lord, how manifold are thy works! in wisdom hast thou made them all," (ver. 24.)

There is, indeed, a mistrust of social science, the youngest daughter of philosophy; a mistrust partly reasonable and partly unreasonable. And perhaps the Christian preacher could not set himself a more appropriate task for this occasion than that of examining the grounds of this mistrust. And first let me speak of the unreasonable form of it.

a. To many persons the notion of law seems to imply necessity. Whilst social facts remain scattered, and are observed singly or in small groups, there seems to be ample scope for our free agency, for our efforts to amend and alter the condition of those around us; but when the facts are bound up into a law, then there appears an iron uniformity which seems to constrain our hands and feet, and make us powerless. Lo! there is an average of convictions for crime, of drunkenness, of ignorance, of mortality of children; and do what we will, the next year will resemble this. We can calculate the cases of theft or murder in the same way that we do the rainfall or the yield of corn. Where, then, is man's free agency, if his destined column in the table of observations is sure to be filled up? Is not he whom we thought free, bound to the chariot of a sure and inevitable destiny—the slave of circumstances under a delusion that he is free? Thinking thus, men associate the laws of social progress with fatalism and materialism in philosophy, and with despair in action.

Yet how can this be? Laws are but facts classified and sorted. It is impossible that it can be hurtful to know facts exactly, if it is good to know them with less precision. There can be no mischief in classifying facts, if there is none in observing them singly and without arrangement. We all expect, in a loose and inexact way, that crimes will be committed, that men will die of want, that there is much ignorance around us. We never, to preserve the rights of our free-will, think it necessary to deny any of these things. Nor need we be afraid, then, to know them in the completest way, and to ascertain that for years past the average number of cases of each crime have been just so many, and the want has found just so many victims, and the dark ranks of ignorance have found just so many recruits. Were these figures quite uniform from year to year—which is of course an impossible supposition—I do not see that this would destroy the individual's power of choice. Say that in a given city three murderers should be found each year, and that all legislation and police failed to make the number greater or less, the necessity would only affect the total ; and it would be conceivable still that one who had raised the dagger for slaughter might draw it back in pity for the smiling helplessness of sleep, whilst another, choosing the drink that steals away men's brains, chose murder with it unawares, and in the flush of passion which he had courted slew his enemy. There would be room for the play of individual choice and motives even if they produced but one sure and uniform result. And a large class of facts, which would have an equal claim with all other facts to the attention of the social philosopher, would still attest man's freedom—the deterring power of punishment, self-control, the stimulus of rewards and honours, the perpetual assumption in every social system that man is not the child of necessity, but amenable to motives.

But the supposition that social results are absolutely uniform has no foundation. The statistics of crime and want are different in England and Scotland, and in the same county but in different years. Even now, in the newness of social science, great alterations become discernible ; for example, in the average duration of life, which has been lengthened by temperance and by more enlight-

ened notions of physiology. The reformatory
school has its averages of those who are saved from
a life of crime and of those who have relapsed.
These exact summaries of facts, instead of paralysing the exertions of the charitable, enable them
to realise the precise amount of effect they have
produced. Have we diminished by one-tenth or
one-twentieth the number of the thoroughly untaught? Have we rescued only two or three
in a hundred from a course of vice? Then the
science that helps me to appreciate my gains
precisely, gives me the greatest encouragement to
proceed in the work of love, emancipates me from
many depressing influences in showing me that the
progress, if slow, is substantial. But it *is* slow!
Yes: therein the results of science coincide with
the lax impressions of common observers. No one
save the enthusiast hopes to alter deep-rooted
social symptoms by a sudden remedy. But science
delivers us from a fanciful estimate of our own success, that varies with our temper and our mood;
refuses to let the sanguine mind cherish his dream
that he has already reformed the world, and cheers
the faint-hearted with the assurance of some fruit.
It assures us of man's freedom at the same time
that it shows that this freedom is exercised in cer-

tain limits. But of these limits we were all aware. We know that no exertions of ours will eradicate want, and want increases temptation, want implies ignorance; and there will always therefore be a residuum of crime upon which our exertions would seem to be powerless. We know that youth, climate, profession, have each its bias. We know that habit is so strong that no nation or place will change its customs in a moment. All this is part of the ordinary man's observation, which he records, not in a scientific form, but in wise saws and homely proverbs. We all know that in our prison house our walk must take a narrow range. But science assures me of the space at my command. So far, then, is she from paralysing my powers, that she encourages me with real successes, and ascertains for me the mass of evil on which I am still to operate.

Another cause of mistrust lies in a certain jealousy which good men feel lest the providence of God should seem to be excluded by the process of reducing social symptoms to fixed rules. Accustomed to see invariable laws of nature in all other parts of creation, we think that with the wills and conduct of our race God deals more freely, and does not bind Himself, if I may say so, by laws and second causes. But, surely, whether the Most High acts upon the heart of a man by means which He has provided, or directly by a voice from above, makes no difference as to His power or the boundless freedom of its exercise. God calls you to Him when the Bible that you read touches your conscience, or some calamity sobers your thoughtless spirit, or the preacher's message seems to have been shaped for your case. God calls you when pious parents guide you towards the good, and take pains to place you so that only good influences may shine over your path with their benign light. You may bless God for protecting you from evil, although the laws of man's making, and customs of decency and sobriety that have grown up long since without a reference to you, are the hedges round about that keep you safe. The Bible, the preacher, the teacher, the parents, the free polity, the good example are all His workmanship: He is near you in these signs and images and instruments of good. And social science does not profess to follow the heart into the sanctuary of God. She deals with outward facts and influences only. "The king's heart," says the wise man, "is in the hand of the Lord, as the river of water: he turneth

it whithersoever he will," (Prov. xxi. 1.) Rules
and calculations do not follow you when in the
temple of your own heart you seek God in prayer,
and perceive your will made stronger and your
mind refreshed as with the evening dew. To
that secret mystery no research can reach; to the
power of choice with which man is endowed, and
the mode in which it is acted upon by Him who
gave it. We surround the mind with good influences which assist the will; but these are not
the will. Calls and arguments are addressed to
it; but though these are heaped up and multi-
plied, we cannot predict that at a certain time
the laden scale will turn. No; the personality of
man asserts itself in this. Those who saw Jesus
suffer and die without a sign of relenting were
melted into sorrow and contrition by Peter's
preaching after Jesus had departed. Saul the
persecutor passed into Paul the apostle by no
gradation that can be expressed in rules. It is
the same in every age. Great missions are undertaken, great ideas diffused, by some one man,
who, unable to analyse his own conviction, has
formed a settled purpose, to which all the lower
elements of society adjust themselves.

And this brings me to the second and more

reasonable ground of mistrust of social science.
Science has ever been ambitious. The swelling
pretensions which Bacon rebuked in the scholastic
philosophy are not more lofty than those which
the Baconian philosophy has frequently put forward since. Histories have been written from
which the mention of God's holy name and of the
free agency of man have been excluded. Schemes
of philosophy have been drawn up from which
theology is banished, as a foe to all exactness and
all progress. In such cases, the real objection and
cause of enmity is, that the facts in that region are
hard to classify, and are beyond the reach of laws
at present known to us. No fair man of any school
will deny that the love of God is a real principle in
many hearts; that belief in a religious truth is the
spring of action of many brave and useful lives;
that the Redeemer of our race guides and governs
us at this very hour, by His word and wish, many
a faithful follower; that He is a felt presence in
many a household; that He writes His name upon
our laws, and has prompted the founding of many
of our institutions. But the one fact which theology accepts, and which science cannot explain, is
the existence of sin in a world of order, and the
consequent need of a special remedy for sin. Sin

cannot be dealt with as one fact amongst many, all
essential to the world's constitution, all alike accepted by Him who orders the world. The Psalmist's eye, after surveying, in the Psalm before us,
all the creation in its close relation to its Maker,
comes back at last to the one outstanding exception that resists this law of obedience, and says,
" Let the sinner be consumed out of the earth, and
let the wicked be no more." Of them alone he
cannot speak as messengers, or ministers, or even
works of God ; and in the spirit of the law he
would have them consumed out of the earth. But
Jesus in the gospel would consume their sin out of
the earth, that sin which is now, as ever, a blot
upon the beautiful Cosmos—order—of the whole.
Hereafter we may know why sin is permitted ;
there must be laws to which it also is subject. But
in the meantime the danger is that, treating it like
other social ingredients, to be dealt with by purely
social means, we abate our horror of sin, as a resistance and defiance of God, and lower our conception of the Redeemer's work, which was to reconcile the sinner to his Father in heaven, that man,
too, purged from his self-will and selfishness, might
be, like all the rest of creation, an obedient minister of the divine will. There is room enough for

all the generalisations of science without being
jealous of religion.   Education, sound and equal
laws, public health, the intercourse of nations, the
reformation of criminals; there is not one of these
subjects in which the minister of religion has not
an equal interest with the social reformer.   The
Christian minister cannot do his work upon an untaught brutish mind, smarting under the oppression
of a bad government, amidst every influence depressing to health, and surrounded by a criminal
or vicious population.   The cure of these evils,
then, is an essential condition of the Christian
teacher's success; but it cannot stand instead of
Christian truth.   It is perhaps a natural mistake;
at all events, it has been made more than once in
modern times, that this machinery is the whole of
social wisdom, and that religion impedes its orderly
arrangement, and should be left on one side.   No:
the fear of the Lord is the beginning of wisdom;
and that fear consists in a knowledge of God by
means of His word, and of a hatred of the sin
which He has so strongly condemned.   It is beyond
calculation how much these averages of crime and
intemperance, so fixed and settled in the result,
have been swayed by the force of the word of
Christ, from the pulpit, from the mother's lips,

from the written page of the Bible. In the result, three, or ten, or a hundred have fallen. But one whose name is there had every opportunity for escape, and yet would sin. Another, whose name is absent from the list, was plucked back from the brink of peril by a timely word of warning. A third fell by reason of the miserable influences by which he was surrounded. A fourth is the victim of hereditary taint. Amidst these struggles of humanity is the function of the Christian teacher. To hold up Jesus as a pattern of life, who has attracted many to love Him in all ages by the very beauty of holiness, and whose example is even now powerful for good ; to warn men of the wages of sin ; to utter the right counsel honestly in a moment of temptation—these are the means by which the Christian minister influences those results that science collects and reasons upon. There is room enough for us and you. Let not science, when she counts the slain, forget the various warriors that shared the battle. Had the Christian minister been silent, the loss would have been greater ; had he laboured more abundantly, (oh, that we may all remember this!) the lists would have been lightened of many a lost one. To the end of time, men will be touched by the message of Christ, and say,

"What shall we do to be saved?" To the end of time men will be kept chaste, and honest, and sober, by the mere wish to please their heavenly Father, when no other considerations would have restrained them. The secret of this divine operation on human spirits refuses to be tabulated, or insulated and laid bare; but it is a fact as sure as that crimes are done, or that ignorance leads to vice.

But if the minister of Christ and the social philosopher can consent to recognise each other's functions, and to forego mutual prejudices, there is much that they can do in common. Their common purpose is to organise the works of Christian love, to count the loss and gain, to learn where suffering presses hard and ignorance debases, and to soothe and solace, instruct and elevate. They are agreed that in the world which God created evil should not be. The Christian minister needs to check and arrest first impressions by the deliberate observations of the philosopher. The philosopher needs the kindly influence of the minister to clothe in words of love the somewhat hard doctrines which he enounces, and to commend them to those for whom they are intended. Their work is one and the same, and they may help one another. Both are, or should be, servants of the King of all the earth, who has made all things in His wisdom. Both are, or should be, ministers of the loving Master who compassionates all our race, who, in the form of a servant, felt social wrongs and was oppressed by man's injustice, who suffered being tempted, and therefore is able to succour them that are tempted, who once would have gathered the children of Jerusalem together, as a hen gathereth her chickens under her wings, and now would fain gather all men together to embrace them with the arms of His love, if they would come to Him, that the world of man might be filled with light, and life, and justice, and peace; that upon the great harp of nature, the string of man that alone jangles, out of tune and harsh, might be adjusted to the universal harmony. "O Lord, how manifold are thy works! in wisdom hast thou made them all : the earth is full of thy riches."

XVI.

CAIN'S QUESTION.

PREACHED IN WESTMINSTER ABBEY, JUNE 23, 1867

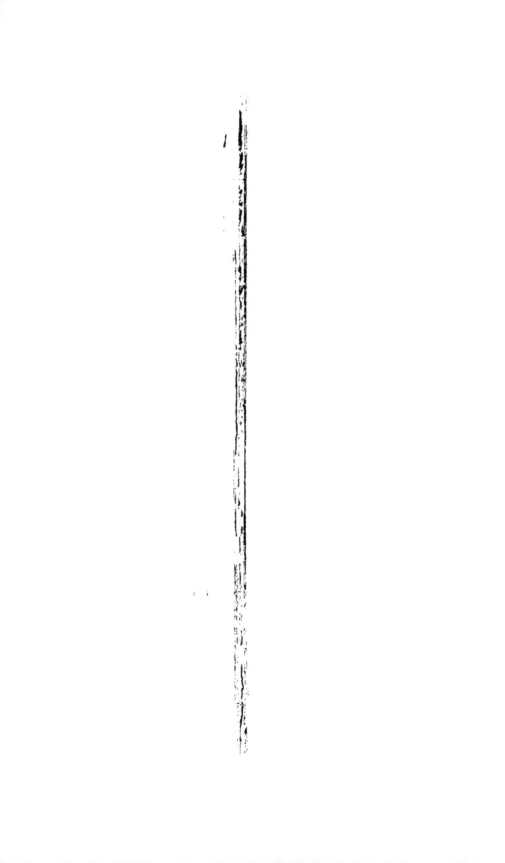

"Am I my brother's keeper?"

CAIN and Abel were trying to do honour to
God, by the mode universal in all old re-
ligions, whether true or false, by offering to God
the things they valued most. By some means, we
know not what, God made known to Cain that his
offering was not accepted. His heart was not right
in it, and sin lay at the door. I suppose there was
some real devotion in what he did, for there was no
one to compel him to offer. But there was more
selfishness than devotion; and when the calculation
failed, and the offering was not repaid in blessing,
selfishness turned to hate, and at some chance
meeting in the field he smote his brother, and invented death. Sin had entered into the world, and
now death entered by sin. Then remorse woke up.
The Lord, speaking this time perhaps in the man's
heart, by a voice not uttered but plain to be
understood, asked him for his brother. "Am I my

brother's keeper?" But the blood that cried to the Lord from the ground was crying also from the ground of the murderer's heart. He saw that exile from man and from God, and death in return for death, awaited him. And he went into the land of Nod, which signifies the land of wandering.

"Am I my brother's keeper?" This is the very gospel of selfishness, and a murderer is its first preacher. Now-a-days it is preached in various forms, not by murderers, but by those who seek the good of their kind. The gospel of selfishness is, that a man must take care of his own interests; and out of that universal self-seeking, provided it be wise and restrained, will come the wellbeing of all. The gospel of God is of a different tone,— "Holy Father, keep through thine own name those whom thou hast given me, that they may be one, as we are. . . . And for their sakes I sanctify myself [offer myself,] that they also might be sanctified through the truth," (John xvii. 11, 19.) Christ regarded men as given into His hand for safe keeping. And to make them holy and at peace with God, He consecrated, or as we read, sanctified Himself upon the cross; and so departed, leaving them this new commandment, binding them for ever, that as He had loved them, so they were to love one another. And in our present social condition there are too many signs of the evil effects of the system of selfishness, both in its higher and more philosophical forms, and in its grosser and more sinful. I propose to-night to speak of some of these evil results. May God be with us, and bring good out of my words, both to you that hear and to me that speak.

Although it is true that rights and duties go together, and that what it is the duty of one to do it is the right of another to receive, it makes the greatest difference in the consequences whether men are trained to regard themselves as owing duties or as claiming rights. You can suppose a well-balanced mind, to whom it would be indifferent whether you appealed to rights or to duties, to whom it would not occur to make any claim for himself without at the same time scrupulously estimating the duties that that same claim entailed upon him. But such minds are not common; and, more or less, men fall into this contradiction, that they expect others to behave with justice, consideration, even with love, towards them, whilst they themselves are guided in dealing with others by motives of self-interest. Rights and duties do in theory go together; every duty viewed on the

the obverse side is a right, and every right a duty.
But then it falls to one's conscience to observe
duties, whilst self-interest takes care of one's rights.
And because conscience is weak and flagging, and
requires help, whilst self-interest needs restraint, it
makes the greatest difference whether a man learns
morals through his duties or his rights.   Inculcate
duty to the exclusion of all mention of rights and
claims, still the spirit of selfishness will not allow
rights to be forgotten.   But teach a man exclusively to be jealous of his rights, and the feeble inward calls of duty may be quite forgotten, and the
naked creed of selfishness may be wholly adopted.
"We will take care of ourselves ; our brethren
must do the same.   Am I my brother's keeper ?"

Now this is an age of rights rather than of
duties.   In saying this one does not of necessity
impute blame.   An age of loud assertion of rights
generally follows an age in which duties have been
neglected.   If the sweet and gracious voice of
conscience does not speak to concede what duty
orders, then the harsher voice of self-interest from
the other side will presently demand it.   An ex-
pensive organisation for shortening the hours and
raising the wages of labour, may have for one of
its causes that hours have been long and wages

scanty in times past. But it is a fact which admits of no dispute, that the common opinion at present takes more account of rights than of duties. The rights of labour, equal political rights, rights of woman ; such are the subjects of the time. It is very notable that there is almost nothing about rights in the teaching of Christ. The disciples are likely to suffer persecution ; but this is predicted with no denunciation of those that are to torment and kill the guiltless. No: He says, " Blessed are they which are persecuted for righteousness' sake. . . . He that endureth to the end shall be saved," (Matt. v. 10; xxiv. 13.) And so with other things. The Lord seeks to train the spirit of His followers into doing and suffering aright. And yet I think that no one would contend that this one-sided system of teaching has done nothing for the recognition of human rights. By all that it has done to show how dear and precious to God every human soul is,—by all its assertions that God judges not with man's eyes, but exalts the lowly and abases them that seem so high,—by its making the poor and maimed and leprous the objects of the tenderest interest and love of the highest Christian minds, —it has done more for human rights by preach-

U

ing only duty than all other systems put together.
What were the poor before Christ's message came?
Slaves of the rich. What were the sick? *Delivered* over to death. There was not an hospital
in the world. What were women? In a worse
sense, slaves. Ah! by preaching love and duty,
and by saying almost nothing of rights, the
Gospel has been the lawgiver of nations, the friend
of man, the champion of his rights. Its teaching
has been of God, of duty, and of love; and where-
ever these ideas have come, freedom and earthly
happiness and cultivation have followed silently
behind.

Here, then, are two systems professing to reach
the same end, but by different roads. Which of
them does this country stand most in need of at
this moment?

It stands in need of that system in which, and
in which alone, religion and morality are inseparably joined together. It stands in need of that
system in which faith in God suggests to us our
duties, whilst in that awful presence the notion of
rights vanishes from the mind. It needs to be
reminded that in one sense each of us has the
keeping of his brethren confided to him, and that
love is the law and the fulfilling of the law. It

stands in need, then, of the Gospel; for these conditions are satisfied nowhere else. From several
quarters the enemies of this system are advancing
against it. Our age is so luxurious, there are so
many who are exempt from the need of labour,
that mere amusement has become the whole business of many young men in the more conspicuous
classes of society. What room is there for the
idea of duty in a life whose amusements fill up the
whole calendar of the year? How can God ever
be invoked in earnest to inspect a life given up to
mere indulgence, even of the less vicious kinds?
He would not bless it; and the sacred gift of
time can be squandered with other help than His.
" If any man love the world, the love of the Father
is not in him," (1 John ii. 15.) Then, on another
side, the mind of this age has become very critical.
It loves certainty, and not such certainty as faith
gives. It would examine the miracles of the
Gospel by a commission of learned societies; it
has no admiration for the sudden outburst of light
from Bethlehem, until it can see all the causes
behind it, and explain that that great *One* came
from a combination of many nothings. All this
tends to limit us more and more to what can be
seen and felt; and we refuse to own that much of

what is seen and felt—nay, all that is best of it—
depends upon an ever-present life of God in us;
that without faith no truth can be held fast, no
good thing heartily desired, no will turned strongly
towards high and holy aims. Then our thoughts
are more concerned with the race of men than
with the individual man. Individual guilt and
merit and suffering are lost sight of by the philosopher, who thinks that in spite of them, ay, and
through them, the race of mankind is marching
on in its irresistible progress towards perfection.
All these elements,—our self-indulgent worldliness, our need of what is called positive truth, the
very form which our sympathy with men has
taken,—conspire to draw us away from God, and
from those duties to men which are the very
essence of Gospel morals. And when the thought
of God recedes, the worship of self replaces it. A.
creed of selfishness tacitly grows up. In its best
form it is a belief that if all men claim their rights
and fight for themselves, the race of men will rise
step by step in well-being; and that the glorious
progress of the whole will be reflected upon the
units that compose it; and that it were mere waste
of time to attempt to minister to individual sin or
sorrow, for these are not evil, but transitions to

good.   In its worst form it is mere greed and luxury.   " Let us eat and drink, for to-morrow we die," (1 Cor. xv. 32.)   There are many phases between ; but from all you might hear the same question, now in supercilious denial, now in carelessness, " Am I my brother's keeper ? "

" Am I my brother's keeper ?"   Say you have staked thousands on a horse-race.   Those thousands are your own ; you can afford to lose them. What have you to do with the poor wretches, who, aping their betters in a fashionable vice, stake what they do not possess, and make good their losses by wronging some trust ?   Are you your brother's keeper ?   Well, if you are not, do not follow the wretch into the scene of his detection, for it may be horrible.   It means punishment and ruin, and even death to him.   He perished, as it would seem, because he was led into sin ; but then there is this strange paradox—that nobody led him.   No one owns that he has had any share in bringing this burden upon his shoulder, by putting forth so much as one finger to lighten it.

" Am I my brother's keeper ?"   The young girl carrying home her work sees as she passes the young man, whose looks and dress proclaim him to her foolish eyes the spoilt darling of a higher sphere of life, leaning easily on the rail, and without a thought of shame, tossing to and fro the joke and laugh with one whose life is a public shame. Once she sees it with a shock. Twice she sees it; thrice she sees, and custom now has staled it, and there is no shock. By and by work grows slack, and hunger presses. She can no longer bear the punishment which society imposes, as it seems, on innocence. She lifts the latch and steps out, to return no more to any home where industry and purity dwell together. And what is that old story to you? Are you your sister's keeper? May you not amuse yourself as others do? To whom are you responsible? Well, if there be question of amusement, you must follow this history no further. For the difference between what she was and what she is to be is unspeakable; and perhaps some human feeling might awaken in you at the contemplation of that contrast which might be painful to the last degree.

These consequences, you will say, are remote, and you did not think of them; but they are worth a thought. For so our God has made us, that sometimes fresh powers of vision come upon us. Though there have gathered over us thick clouds of human notions that hide the sky and make things round us dim, those clouds may be riven, and an intolerable light from on high shine out, and things around us may show out in truer shapes. And as a man who passed safely in the dark along a perilous ledge, with death within three inches, fainted the next day when he revisited the place, at the very reflection of his danger, so might you see in this new light links of responsibility uniting you to the lost, and a brotherhood with them in their ruin, —nay, possibly a conviction that Cain's question, behind which you sat so strong, is utterly futile, because Christ has given you to keep all that your hand can reach among your brethren. "Where is thy brother?" "I know not. He was given into my hand to keep, and I have lost him."

Take one case more. Within the last week* a few lines have been added to the history of this country, which will probably never be blotted out; they are too necessary to explain some facts in the history of our people. There has grown up a law of wages among us, not written in any book of laws, but potent, and also severe, for the penalty of transgressing it is death. One of the deadly sins under this code is hiring a youth to work, and

---

* Written just after the disclosure of the Sheffield Trades Union murders and outrages.

paying him for it ; and for that the punishment is
death. Fifteen pieces of gold reward the execu-
tioner, surely no great sum for the vigilance of
weeks, and for a sure aim at last. It is for the
good of the whole trade that wages should be kept
up, and this hiring of cheap labour of youths is
fatal, if not checked. The man must die, then he
will hire no more youths, and the interests and
rights of a great class be protected. Oh, poor distracted brother, if you could have continued to the
end the monster of wickedness you have made
yourself, we should have lost the awful lesson you
have taught us. But God exists, and, under all
the sin that has marred your heart, there remains
a conscience still capable of remorse. You thought
you were not your brother's keeper ; that his life
was nothing to you compared with the interest of
you and of others. But when the old story of
murder is revived, is looked into by judicial eyes
of men who know not your gospel of wages, and
still remember, " Thou shalt not kill," then your
conscience wakes to answer them. There swoon-
ing under the weight of the truth which you are
yet constrained to utter,—clutching at your throat,
they say, as though the blood of the victim was
choking you,—you have found at last that venal

murder has its punishment. Men have set a mark on you, as God did on Cain ; none shall destroy you, though you were pitiless to destroy. But to me you are a witness of the presence and power of God. "Am I my brother's keeper?" Yes; for the weight of his death presses so heavily on your heart.

None of us can remark this disorder in our social state without disquiet ; yet it is the sickness of the strong man. There is much life in him, much vigour, perchance he shall not die ; but when you tell him that the Bible contains the cure, he answers that the morals of the New Testament have yielded to his generation all that they can yield, and that its dogmas are effete. I say, once more, that the morality cannot be severed from the dogma : " Herein is love, not that we loved God, but that he loved us, and sent his Son to be the propitiation for our sins. Beloved, if God so loved us, we ought also to love one another," (1 John iv. 10, 11.) Here the rights of men to our love, to our consideration, rest upon an act of divine love. You recognise these rights; but the fact of revelation, which first proclaimed their admission, you think can be dispensed with ; yet no other religion or philosophy ever set men so high. Their chartered right to our reverence is in these terms: "That God loved them, and sent his Son to be the propitiation for their sins;" and the Saviour set to it His seal, and signed it with His blood. You do not like this supernatural origin, and will rest upon something else; but already the punishment of this begins. If these rights, for which you contend, are the right of man to spend his soul in idleness and excitement, and of women to be destroyed, and of children to go untaught, and of the artisan to make rules restraining his brother artisan from his rights on pain of blood, then it is useless to contend for the supernatural origin of a charter such as this. But these signal failures and contradictions are just the consequence of the separation you are trying to make between religion and conduct. Because you have left no place for the Saviour in your scheme, your plan for humanity is crumbling away: a humanity that does not protect you from sensuality and worldliness such as no class can long survive—a humanity which will march on to realise its selfish notions even through blood—is condemned already. Call back into your life the Saviour Christ, who alone in the world's history has shown Himself the Lord King, able to bind human society together. Pray

Him to resume for you the work which philosophy has been spoiling. Bow down before Him, when He tells us through His apostle, "If we love one another, God dwelleth in us, and his love is perfected in us," (1 John iv. 12.) In deference to modern fashions, you have banished from your speech and thought such ideas as faith, and prayer, and humble reverence, and a trust in providence, and fear of sin. And thus, with feet twisted and compressed, you have striven to walk along a path where only free feet can walk. Give full scope now to all your nature. Men tell you that the part of you that belongs to earth is alone real, and the part that leads you towards heaven belongs to the region of sentiments and dreams. Not so. Faith and love are heavenly things, but they are earthly too. These two elements make the salt of the earth, for want of which society is breaking already into spots of corruption. The poet speaks to his friend—

> "I would the great world grew like thee
> That grewest not alone in power
> And knowledge, but from hour to hour
> In reverence and in charity."

A man pluming himself, and congratulating his fellows on the power and knowledge they have achieved, thus deifying himself by tacitly taking his share of that admiration that he bestows on his wonderful species, is a sorry spectacle at best. But there is something nobler in him, and at unexpected moments the Lord speaks, as to Cain, and another world starts forth for him, and he sees that his life, conducted on approved principles too, with no scandals, with much money, much ease, and a reasonable share of men's good-will, has been a lie, and a cruelty, and a waste. Dismiss these grand vague schemes of improvement and progress, and begin from the foundation. Men expect that by neglecting the individuals, and vindicating the rights of the race, a race pure and frugal, temperate and chaste, will rise up. As if the tower could be stronger or better than the materials that compose it ; as if a marble edifice could be formed from dust and slime. Find work for yourself amongst those of your fellow-men that surround you. You are their keeper. I had almost said that you may stand to them in the Saviour's place, " because as he is, so are we in this world," (1 John iv. 17.) Carry to the lips that are nearest you the cup of guidance and consolation. Think each day whether you are doing aught, whether vicious or only questionable, that may have harmed your brother. For you, your own part is enough; God reserves for Himself, out of the lively stones that you and many shall prepare for Him, the construction of the great living temple to His own honour. Enough for you and me—nay, more than enough, unspeakable joy and triumph—to be able to say, when the Lord asks "Where is thy brother?" "Of them which thou gavest me, have I lost none," (John xviii. 9.)

THE END.

Ballantyne and Company, Printers, Edinburgh.

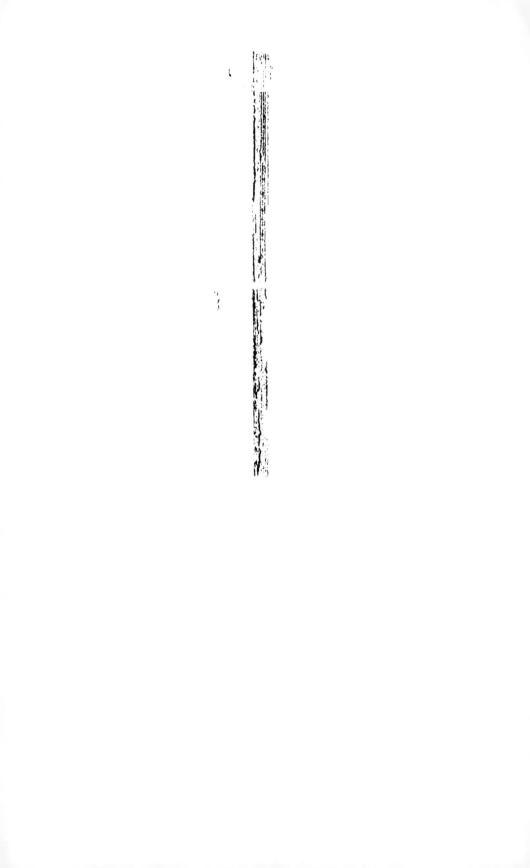

RECENT WORKS.

An Address on the Confirmation of H.R.H. Prince Arthur. By the LORD ARCHBISHOP OF CANTERBURY. 8vo, 1s.

Sermons Preached in Lincoln's Inn Chapel. By the LORD ARCHBISHOP OF YORK. 8vo, 10s. 6d..

Aids to Faith: A Series of Theological Essays. Edited by the LORD ARCHBISHOP OF YORK. 8vo, 9s.

CONTENTS.

Miracles....................................Canon MANSEL, B.D.
Evidences of Christianity.....................BISHOP OF KILLALOE.
*Prophecy & Mosaic Record of Creation.*Dr M'CAUL.
Ideology and Subscription...................Canon COOK, M.A.
The Pentateuch..............................GEORGE RAWLINSON, M.A.
Inspiration..................................BISHOP OF ELY.
Death of Christ.............................ARCHBISHOP OF YORK.
Scripture and its Interpretation.........BISHOP OF GLOUCESTER AND BRISTOL.

On the Insuperable Differences which Separate the Church of England from the Church of Rome. By the LORD BISHOP OF EXETER. New Edition. Post 8vo, 7s. 6d.

A Memoir of Charles James Blomfield, D.D., Lord Bishop of London. With Selections from his Correspondence. Edited by his Son. With Portrait. Post 8vo, 12s.

Sermons Preached before the University of Oxford. By Rev. ROBERT SCOTT, D.D., Master of Baliol College, and Professor of the Exegesis of Holy Scripture, Oxford. Post 8vo, 8s. 6d.

Sermons Preached in Lincoln's Inn Chapel, and on Special Occasions. By Canon COOK, M.A., Preacher to the Honourable Society of Lincoln's Inn. 8vo, 9s.

Meditations on the Religious Questions of the Day. Part I. The Essence of Christianity. Part II. Present State of Christianity. By M. GUIZOT. 2 vols. post 8vo, 20s.

The Messiah: A Narrative of the Life, Death, Resurrection, and Ascension of our Lord; in the Chronological Order of the Four Gospels. By a Layman. Map. 8vo, 18s.

Life of Thomas Ken, Bishop of Bath and Wells. By a Layman. 2 vols. 8vo, 18s.

The Limits of Religious Thought. By Canon MANSEL, B.D. 5th Edition, with New Preface. Post 8vo, 8s. 6d.

Historical Evidences of the Truth of the Scripture Records stated anew, with Special Reference to the Doubts and Discoveries of Modern Times. By Rev. GEORGE RAW-LINSON, M.A. 2d Edition. 8vo, 14s.

*Sunday; its Origin, History, and Present Obliga-*tions Considered. By Rev. J. A. HESSEY, D.C.L. 3d Edition. Post 8vo, 9s.

A Critical History of Free Thought in reference to the Christian Religion. By Rev. A. S. FARRAR, M.A. 8vo, 16s.

Relation between the Divine and Human Elements in Holy Scripture. By Rev. J. HANNAH, D.C.L. 8vo, 10s. 6d.

Undesigned Coincidences in the Writings of the Old and New Testaments, an Argument of their Veracity. By Rev. J. J. BLUNT, B.D. 9th Edition. Post 8vo, 6s.

Benedicite; or, The Song of the Three Children. Being Illustrations of the Power, Wisdom, and Goodness of the Creator. By G. C. CHILD, M.D. 2 vols. fcp. 8vo, 12s.

*The Continuity of Scripture as Declared by the Tes-*timony of our Lord and of the Evangelists and Apostles. By By SIR WM. PAGE WOOD, F.R.S. Post 8vo, 6s.

Hymns Written and Adapted to the Weekly Church Service of the Year. By Bishop HEBER. 16mo, 1s. 6d.

The Illustrated New Testament. Edited, with a. short Practical Commentary for Family Use, by Archdeacon CHURTON, M.A., and Archdeacon BASIL JONES, M.A. With 100 authentic Illustrations and 8 Panoramic Views. 2 vols. crown 8vo, 30s.

The Illustrated Prayer-Book. With Ornamental Scrolls, Foliage, Head-pieces, Borders, Initial Letters, and 40 Historical Engravings. Edited by Rev. THOMAS JAMES, M.A. 8vo, 18s.

JOHN MURRAY, ALBEMARLE STREET.